C-1429   CAREER EXAMINATION SERIES

This is your
PASSBOOK for...

Probation Officer Trainee

Test Preparation Study Guide
Questions & Answers

COPYRIGHT NOTICE

This book is SOLELY intended for, is sold ONLY to, and its use is RESTRICTED to individual, bona fide applicants or candidates who qualify by virtue of having seriously filed applications for appropriate license, certificate, professional and/or promotional advancement, higher school matriculation, scholarship, or other legitimate requirements of education and/or governmental authorities.

This book is NOT intended for use, class instruction, tutoring, training, duplication, copying, reprinting, excerption, or adaptation, etc., by:

1) Other publishers
2) Proprietors and/or Instructors of "Coaching" and/or Preparatory Courses
3) Personnel and/or Training Divisions of commercial, industrial, and governmental organizations
4) Schools, colleges, or universities and/or their departments and staffs, including teachers and other personnel
5) Testing Agencies or Bureaus
6) Study groups which seek by the purchase of a single volume to copy and/or duplicate and/or adapt this material for use by the group as a whole without having purchased individual volumes for each of the members of the group
7) Et al.

Such persons would be in violation of appropriate Federal and State statutes.

PROVISION OF LICENSING AGREEMENTS – Recognized educational, commercial, industrial, and governmental institutions and organizations, and others legitimately engaged in educational pursuits, including training, testing, and measurement activities, may address request for a licensing agreement to the copyright owners, who will determine whether, and under what conditions, including fees and charges, the materials in this book may be used them. In other words, a licensing facility exists for the legitimate use of the material in this book on other than an individual basis. However, it is asseverated and affirmed here that the material in this book CANNOT be used without the receipt of the express permission of such a licensing agreement from the Publishers. Inquiries re licensing should be addressed to the company, attention rights and permissions department.

All rights reserved, including the right of reproduction in whole or in part, in any form or by any means, electronic or mechanical, including photocopying, recording, or by any information storage and retrieval system, without permission in writing from the Publisher.

Copyright © 2024 by
National Learning Corporation

212 Michael Drive, Syosset, NY 11791
(516) 921-8888 • www.passbooks.com
E-mail: info@passbooks.com

PUBLISHED IN THE UNITED STATES OF AMERICA

PASSBOOK® SERIES

THE *PASSBOOK® SERIES* has been created to prepare applicants and candidates for the ultimate academic battlefield – the examination room.

At some time in our lives, each and every one of us may be required to take an examination – for validation, matriculation, admission, qualification, registration, certification, or licensure.

Based on the assumption that every applicant or candidate has met the basic formal educational standards, has taken the required number of courses, and read the necessary texts, the *PASSBOOK® SERIES* furnishes the one special preparation which may assure passing with confidence, instead of failing with insecurity. Examination questions – together with answers – are furnished as the basic vehicle for study so that the mysteries of the examination and its compounding difficulties may be eliminated or diminished by a sure method.

This book is meant to help you pass your examination provided that you qualify and are serious in your objective.

The entire field is reviewed through the huge store of content information which is succinctly presented through a provocative and challenging approach – the question-and-answer method.

A climate of success is established by furnishing the correct answers at the end of each test.

You soon learn to recognize types of questions, forms of questions, and patterns of questioning. You may even begin to anticipate expected outcomes.

You perceive that many questions are repeated or adapted so that you can gain acute insights, which may enable you to score many sure points.

You learn how to confront new questions, or types of questions, and to attack them confidently and work out the correct answers.

You note objectives and emphases, and recognize pitfalls and dangers, so that you may make positive educational adjustments.

Moreover, you are kept fully informed in relation to new concepts, methods, practices, and directions in the field.

You discover that you are actually taking the examination all the time: you are preparing for the examination by "taking" an examination, not by reading extraneous and/or supererogatory textbooks.

In short, this PASSBOOK®, used directedly, should be an important factor in helping you to pass your test.

PROBATION OFFICER TRAINEE

DUTIES:
Probation Officer Trainees, under close supervision, receive a course of in-service training and perform beginning level professional work for the purpose of acquiring knowledge, skill and competence in the field of probation work; and perform related work. Assists in performing professional probation work related to the intake, investigation and supervision functions in the probation department. They conduct court-ordered investigation of criminal offenses; obtain detailed information about the offense, the offender's legal, economic and psycho-social history, and the impact of the offense on the complainant/victim; prepare and submit written reports and recommendations; supervise probationers and provide supportive casework/counseling services; refer probationers to social, government or community agencies or other entities which may assist in the probationer's rehabilitation; perform field work including home visits to probationers; correspond with and make collateral visits to relatives, community agencies and employers; ensure probationers are adhering to the conditions of probation; prepare and maintain case records; may be assigned to specialized units and/or programs; and may operate a motor vehicle.

ESSENTIAL FUNCTIONS:
The following duties are normal for this position. These are not to be construed as exclusive or all-inclusive. Other duties may be required and assigned.
- Confers with offender, legal representatives, family, and other concerned persons and reviews documents regarding offender's legal and social history as a means of conducting preheating or presentencing investigations and to formulate rehabilitation plan.
- Compiles reports, testifies in court and makes recommendations concerning conditional release or institutionalization of offender.
- Informs offender's or guardian of legal requirements of conditional release such visits to office, restitution payments, or educational and employment stipulations.
- Counsels offender and family or guardian. Encourages offender to complete education, secure, employment.
- Arranges custodial care and refers offender to social resources in community to aid in rehabilitation.
- Evaluates offender's progress on follow-up basis including visits to home, school and place of employment.
- Secures remedial action by court if necessary.
- Meets with probationers on a periodic basis to assess progress; prepares progress reports.
- Arranges for placement or clinical services if ordered by court.
- Works with probationers according to treatment plan.
- Refers caseload problems to supervisor for discussion and resolution.

SCOPE OF THE EXAMINATION
The written test will cover knowledge, skills and/or abilities in such areas as:
1. Understanding and interpreting written material;
2. Report writing and record keeping;
3. Interviewing and interpersonal relations; and
4. Evaluating conclusions in light of known facts.

HOW TO TAKE A TEST

I. YOU MUST PASS AN EXAMINATION

A. *WHAT EVERY CANDIDATE SHOULD KNOW*

Examination applicants often ask us for help in preparing for the written test. What can I study in advance? What kinds of questions will be asked? How will the test be given? How will the papers be graded?

As an applicant for a civil service examination, you may be wondering about some of these things. Our purpose here is to suggest effective methods of advance study and to describe civil service examinations.

Your chances for success on this examination can be increased if you know how to prepare. Those "pre-examination jitters" can be reduced if you know what to expect. You can even experience an adventure in good citizenship if you know why civil service exams are given.

B. *WHY ARE CIVIL SERVICE EXAMINATIONS GIVEN?*

Civil service examinations are important to you in two ways. As a citizen, you want public jobs filled by employees who know how to do their work. As a job seeker, you want a fair chance to compete for that job on an equal footing with other candidates. The best-known means of accomplishing this two-fold goal is the competitive examination.

Exams are widely publicized throughout the nation. They may be administered for jobs in federal, state, city, municipal, town or village governments or agencies.

Any citizen may apply, with some limitations, such as the age or residence of applicants. Your experience and education may be reviewed to see whether you meet the requirements for the particular examination. When these requirements exist, they are reasonable and applied consistently to all applicants. Thus, a competitive examination may cause you some uneasiness now, but it is your privilege and safeguard.

C. *HOW ARE CIVIL SERVICE EXAMS DEVELOPED?*

Examinations are carefully written by trained technicians who are specialists in the field known as "psychological measurement," in consultation with recognized authorities in the field of work that the test will cover. These experts recommend the subject matter areas or skills to be tested; only those knowledges or skills important to your success on the job are included. The most reliable books and source materials available are used as references. Together, the experts and technicians judge the difficulty level of the questions.

Test technicians know how to phrase questions so that the problem is clearly stated. Their ethics do not permit "trick" or "catch" questions. Questions may have been tried out on sample groups, or subjected to statistical analysis, to determine their usefulness.

Written tests are often used in combination with performance tests, ratings of training and experience, and oral interviews. All of these measures combine to form the best-known means of finding the right person for the right job.

II. HOW TO PASS THE WRITTEN TEST

A. NATURE OF THE EXAMINATION

To prepare intelligently for civil service examinations, you should know how they differ from school examinations you have taken. In school you were assigned certain definite pages to read or subjects to cover. The examination questions were quite detailed and usually emphasized memory. Civil service exams, on the other hand, try to discover your present ability to perform the duties of a position, plus your potentiality to learn these duties. In other words, a civil service exam attempts to predict how successful you will be. Questions cover such a broad area that they cannot be as minute and detailed as school exam questions.

In the public service similar kinds of work, or positions, are grouped together in one "class." This process is known as *position-classification*. All the positions in a class are paid according to the salary range for that class. One class title covers all of these positions, and they are all tested by the same examination.

B. FOUR BASIC STEPS

1) Study the announcement

How, then, can you know what subjects to study? Our best answer is: "Learn as much as possible about the class of positions for which you've applied." The exam will test the knowledge, skills and abilities needed to do the work.

Your most valuable source of information about the position you want is the official exam announcement. This announcement lists the training and experience qualifications. Check these standards and apply only if you come reasonably close to meeting them.

The brief description of the position in the examination announcement offers some clues to the subjects which will be tested. Think about the job itself. Review the duties in your mind. Can you perform them, or are there some in which you are rusty? Fill in the blank spots in your preparation.

Many jurisdictions preview the written test in the exam announcement by including a section called "Knowledge and Abilities Required," "Scope of the Examination," or some similar heading. Here you will find out specifically what fields will be tested.

2) Review your own background

Once you learn in general what the position is all about, and what you need to know to do the work, ask yourself which subjects you already know fairly well and which need improvement. You may wonder whether to concentrate on improving your strong areas or on building some background in your fields of weakness. When the announcement has specified "some knowledge" or "considerable knowledge," or has used adjectives like "beginning principles of…" or "advanced … methods," you can get a clue as to the number and difficulty of questions to be asked in any given field. More questions, and hence broader coverage, would be included for those subjects which are more important in the work. Now weigh your strengths and weaknesses against the job requirements and prepare accordingly.

3) Determine the level of the position

Another way to tell how intensively you should prepare is to understand the level of the job for which you are applying. Is it the entering level? In other words, is this the position in which beginners in a field of work are hired? Or is it an intermediate or advanced level? Sometimes this is indicated by such words as "Junior" or "Senior" in the class title. Other jurisdictions use Roman numerals to designate the level – Clerk I, Clerk II, for example. The word "Supervisor" sometimes appears in the title. If the level is not indicated by the title, check the description of duties. Will you be working under very close supervision, or will you have responsibility for independent decisions in this work?

4) Choose appropriate study materials

Now that you know the subjects to be examined and the relative amount of each subject to be covered, you can choose suitable study materials. For beginning level jobs, or even advanced ones, if you have a pronounced weakness in some aspect of your training, read a modern, standard textbook in that field. Be sure it is up to date and has general coverage. Such books are normally available at your library, and the librarian will be glad to help you locate one. For entry-level positions, questions of appropriate difficulty are chosen – neither highly advanced questions, nor those too simple. Such questions require careful thought but not advanced training.

If the position for which you are applying is technical or advanced, you will read more advanced, specialized material. If you are already familiar with the basic principles of your field, elementary textbooks would waste your time. Concentrate on advanced textbooks and technical periodicals. Think through the concepts and review difficult problems in your field.

These are all general sources. You can get more ideas on your own initiative, following these leads. For example, training manuals and publications of the government agency which employs workers in your field can be useful, particularly for technical and professional positions. A letter or visit to the government department involved may result in more specific study suggestions, and certainly will provide you with a more definite idea of the exact nature of the position you are seeking.

III. KINDS OF TESTS

Tests are used for purposes other than measuring knowledge and ability to perform specified duties. For some positions, it is equally important to test ability to make adjustments to new situations or to profit from training. In others, basic mental abilities not dependent on information are essential. Questions which test these things may not appear as pertinent to the duties of the position as those which test for knowledge and information. Yet they are often highly important parts of a fair examination. For very general questions, it is almost impossible to help you direct your study efforts. What we can do is to point out some of the more common of these general abilities needed in public service positions and describe some typical questions.

1) General information

Broad, general information has been found useful for predicting job success in some kinds of work. This is tested in a variety of ways, from vocabulary lists to questions about current events. Basic background in some field of work, such as sociology or economics, may be sampled in a group of questions. Often these are principles which have become familiar to most persons through exposure rather than through formal training. It is difficult to advise you how to study for these questions; being alert to the world around you is our best suggestion.

2) Verbal ability

An example of an ability needed in many positions is verbal or language ability. Verbal ability is, in brief, the ability to use and understand words. Vocabulary and grammar tests are typical measures of this ability. Reading comprehension or paragraph interpretation questions are common in many kinds of civil service tests. You are given a paragraph of written material and asked to find its central meaning.

3) Numerical ability

Number skills can be tested by the familiar arithmetic problem, by checking paired lists of numbers to see which are alike and which are different, or by interpreting charts and graphs. In the latter test, a graph may be printed in the test booklet which you are asked to use as the basis for answering questions.

4) Observation

A popular test for law-enforcement positions is the observation test. A picture is shown to you for several minutes, then taken away. Questions about the picture test your ability to observe both details and larger elements.

5) Following directions

In many positions in the public service, the employee must be able to carry out written instructions dependably and accurately. You may be given a chart with several columns, each column listing a variety of information. The questions require you to carry out directions involving the information given in the chart.

6) Skills and aptitudes

Performance tests effectively measure some manual skills and aptitudes. When the skill is one in which you are trained, such as typing or shorthand, you can practice. These tests are often very much like those given in business school or high school courses. For many of the other skills and aptitudes, however, no short-time preparation can be made. Skills and abilities natural to you or that you have developed throughout your lifetime are being tested.

Many of the general questions just described provide all the data needed to answer the questions and ask you to use your reasoning ability to find the answers. Your best preparation for these tests, as well as for tests of facts and ideas, is to be at your physical and mental best. You, no doubt, have your own methods of getting into an exam-taking mood and keeping "in shape." The next section lists some ideas on this subject.

IV. KINDS OF QUESTIONS

Only rarely is the "essay" question, which you answer in narrative form, used in civil service tests. Civil service tests are usually of the short-answer type. Full instructions for answering these questions will be given to you at the examination. But in case this is your first experience with short-answer questions and separate answer sheets, here is what you need to know:

1) Multiple-choice Questions

Most popular of the short-answer questions is the "multiple choice" or "best answer" question. It can be used, for example, to test for factual knowledge, ability to solve problems or judgment in meeting situations found at work.

A multiple-choice question is normally one of three types—
- It can begin with an incomplete statement followed by several possible endings. You are to find the one ending which *best* completes the statement, although some of the others may not be entirely wrong.
- It can also be a complete statement in the form of a question which is answered by choosing one of the statements listed.

- It can be in the form of a problem – again you select the best answer.

Here is an example of a multiple-choice question with a discussion which should give you some clues as to the method for choosing the right answer:

When an employee has a complaint about his assignment, the action which will *best* help him overcome his difficulty is to
   A. discuss his difficulty with his coworkers
   B. take the problem to the head of the organization
   C. take the problem to the person who gave him the assignment
   D. say nothing to anyone about his complaint

In answering this question, you should study each of the choices to find which is best. Consider choice "A" – Certainly an employee may discuss his complaint with fellow employees, but no change or improvement can result, and the complaint remains unresolved. Choice "B" is a poor choice since the head of the organization probably does not know what assignment you have been given, and taking your problem to him is known as "going over the head" of the supervisor. The supervisor, or person who made the assignment, is the person who can clarify it or correct any injustice. Choice "C" is, therefore, correct. To say nothing, as in choice "D," is unwise. Supervisors have and interest in knowing the problems employees are facing, and the employee is seeking a solution to his problem.

2) True/False Questions

The "true/false" or "right/wrong" form of question is sometimes used. Here a complete statement is given. Your job is to decide whether the statement is right or wrong.

SAMPLE: A roaming cell-phone call to a nearby city costs less than a non-roaming call to a distant city.

This statement is wrong, or false, since roaming calls are more expensive.

This is not a complete list of all possible question forms, although most of the others are variations of these common types. You will always get complete directions for answering questions. Be sure you understand *how* to mark your answers – ask questions until you do.

V. RECORDING YOUR ANSWERS

Computer terminals are used more and more today for many different kinds of exams.
For an examination with very few applicants, you may be told to record your answers in the test booklet itself. Separate answer sheets are much more common. If this separate answer sheet is to be scored by machine – and this is often the case – it is highly important that you mark your answers correctly in order to get credit.
An electronic scoring machine is often used in civil service offices because of the speed with which papers can be scored. Machine-scored answer sheets must be marked with a pencil, which will be given to you. This pencil has a high graphite content which responds to the electronic scoring machine. As a matter of fact, stray dots may register as answers, so do not let your pencil rest on the answer sheet while you are pondering the correct answer. Also, if your pencil lead breaks or is otherwise defective, ask for another.

Since the answer sheet will be dropped in a slot in the scoring machine, be careful not to bend the corners or get the paper crumpled.

The answer sheet normally has five vertical columns of numbers, with 30 numbers to a column. These numbers correspond to the question numbers in your test booklet. After each number, going across the page are four or five pairs of dotted lines. These short dotted lines have small letters or numbers above them. The first two pairs may also have a "T" or "F" above the letters. This indicates that the first two pairs only are to be used if the questions are of the true-false type. If the questions are multiple choice, disregard the "T" and "F" and pay attention only to the small letters or numbers.

Answer your questions in the manner of the sample that follows:

32. The largest city in the United States is
    A. Washington, D.C.
    B. New York City
    C. Chicago
    D. Detroit
    E. San Francisco

1) Choose the answer you think is best. (New York City is the largest, so "B" is correct.)
2) Find the row of dotted lines numbered the same as the question you are answering. (Find row number 32)
3) Find the pair of dotted lines corresponding to the answer. (Find the pair of lines under the mark "B.")
4) Make a solid black mark between the dotted lines.

VI. BEFORE THE TEST

Common sense will help you find procedures to follow to get ready for an examination. Too many of us, however, overlook these sensible measures. Indeed, nervousness and fatigue have been found to be the most serious reasons why applicants fail to do their best on civil service tests. Here is a list of reminders:

- Begin your preparation early – Don't wait until the last minute to go scurrying around for books and materials or to find out what the position is all about.
- Prepare continuously – An hour a night for a week is better than an all-night cram session. This has been definitely established. What is more, a night a week for a month will return better dividends than crowding your study into a shorter period of time.
- Locate the place of the exam – You have been sent a notice telling you when and where to report for the examination. If the location is in a different town or otherwise unfamiliar to you, it would be well to inquire the best route and learn something about the building.
- Relax the night before the test – Allow your mind to rest. Do not study at all that night. Plan some mild recreation or diversion; then go to bed early and get a good night's sleep.
- Get up early enough to make a leisurely trip to the place for the test – This way unforeseen events, traffic snarls, unfamiliar buildings, etc. will not upset you.
- Dress comfortably – A written test is not a fashion show. You will be known by number and not by name, so wear something comfortable.

- Leave excess paraphernalia at home – Shopping bags and odd bundles will get in your way. You need bring only the items mentioned in the official notice you received; usually everything you need is provided. Do not bring reference books to the exam. They will only confuse those last minutes and be taken away from you when in the test room.
- Arrive somewhat ahead of time – If because of transportation schedules you must get there very early, bring a newspaper or magazine to take your mind off yourself while waiting.
- Locate the examination room – When you have found the proper room, you will be directed to the seat or part of the room where you will sit. Sometimes you are given a sheet of instructions to read while you are waiting. Do not fill out any forms until you are told to do so; just read them and be prepared.
- Relax and prepare to listen to the instructions
- If you have any physical problem that may keep you from doing your best, be sure to tell the test administrator. If you are sick or in poor health, you really cannot do your best on the exam. You can come back and take the test some other time.

VII. AT THE TEST

The day of the test is here and you have the test booklet in your hand. The temptation to get going is very strong. Caution! There is more to success than knowing the right answers. You must know how to identify your papers and understand variations in the type of short-answer question used in this particular examination. Follow these suggestions for maximum results from your efforts:

1) Cooperate with the monitor

The test administrator has a duty to create a situation in which you can be as much at ease as possible. He will give instructions, tell you when to begin, check to see that you are marking your answer sheet correctly, and so on. He is not there to guard you, although he will see that your competitors do not take unfair advantage. He wants to help you do your best.

2) Listen to all instructions

Don't jump the gun! Wait until you understand all directions. In most civil service tests you get more time than you need to answer the questions. So don't be in a hurry. Read each word of instructions until you clearly understand the meaning. Study the examples, listen to all announcements and follow directions. Ask questions if you do not understand what to do.

3) Identify your papers

Civil service exams are usually identified by number only. You will be assigned a number; you must not put your name on your test papers. Be sure to copy your number correctly. Since more than one exam may be given, copy your exact examination title.

4) Plan your time

Unless you are told that a test is a "speed" or "rate of work" test, speed itself is usually not important. Time enough to answer all the questions will be provided, but this does not mean that you have all day. An overall time limit has been set. Divide the total time (in minutes) by the number of questions to determine the approximate time you have for each question.

5) Do not linger over difficult questions

If you come across a difficult question, mark it with a paper clip (useful to have along) and come back to it when you have been through the booklet. One caution if you do this – be sure to skip a number on your answer sheet as well. Check often to be sure that you have not lost your place and that you are marking in the row numbered the same as the question you are answering.

6) Read the questions

Be sure you know what the question asks! Many capable people are unsuccessful because they failed to *read* the questions correctly.

7) Answer all questions

Unless you have been instructed that a penalty will be deducted for incorrect answers, it is better to guess than to omit a question.

8) Speed tests

It is often better NOT to guess on speed tests. It has been found that on timed tests people are tempted to spend the last few seconds before time is called in marking answers at random – without even reading them – in the hope of picking up a few extra points. To discourage this practice, the instructions may warn you that your score will be "corrected" for guessing. That is, a penalty will be applied. The incorrect answers will be deducted from the correct ones, or some other penalty formula will be used.

9) Review your answers

If you finish before time is called, go back to the questions you guessed or omitted to give them further thought. Review other answers if you have time.

10) Return your test materials

If you are ready to leave before others have finished or time is called, take ALL your materials to the monitor and leave quietly. Never take any test material with you. The monitor can discover whose papers are not complete, and taking a test booklet may be grounds for disqualification.

VIII. EXAMINATION TECHNIQUES

1) Read the general instructions carefully. These are usually printed on the first page of the exam booklet. As a rule, these instructions refer to the timing of the examination; the fact that you should not start work until the signal and must stop work at a signal, etc. If there are any *special* instructions, such as a choice of questions to be answered, make sure that you note this instruction carefully.

2) When you are ready to start work on the examination, that is as soon as the signal has been given, read the instructions to each question booklet, underline any key words or phrases, such as *least, best, outline, describe* and the like. In this way you will tend to answer as requested rather than discover on reviewing your paper that you *listed without describing*, that you selected the *worst* choice rather than the *best* choice, etc.

3) If the examination is of the objective or multiple-choice type – that is, each question will also give a series of possible answers: A, B, C or D, and you are called upon to select the best answer and write the letter next to that answer on your answer paper – it is advisable to start answering each question in turn. There may be anywhere from 50 to 100 such questions in the three or four hours allotted and you can see how much time would be taken if you read through all the questions before beginning to answer any. Furthermore, if you come across a question or group of questions which you know would be difficult to answer, it would undoubtedly affect your handling of all the other questions.

4) If the examination is of the essay type and contains but a few questions, it is a moot point as to whether you should read all the questions before starting to answer any one. Of course, if you are given a choice – say five out of seven and the like – then it is essential to read all the questions so you can eliminate the two that are most difficult. If, however, you are asked to answer all the questions, there may be danger in trying to answer the easiest one first because you may find that you will spend too much time on it. The best technique is to answer the first question, then proceed to the second, etc.

5) Time your answers. Before the exam begins, write down the time it started, then add the time allowed for the examination and write down the time it must be completed, then divide the time available somewhat as follows:
    - If 3-1/2 hours are allowed, that would be 210 minutes. If you have 80 objective-type questions, that would be an average of 2-1/2 minutes per question. Allow yourself no more than 2 minutes per question, or a total of 160 minutes, which will permit about 50 minutes to review.
    - If for the time allotment of 210 minutes there are 7 essay questions to answer, that would average about 30 minutes a question. Give yourself only 25 minutes per question so that you have about 35 minutes to review.

6) The most important instruction is to *read each question* and make sure you know what is wanted. The second most important instruction is to *time yourself properly* so that you answer every question. The third most important instruction is to *answer every question*. Guess if you have to but include something for each question. Remember that you will receive no credit for a blank and will probably receive some credit if you write something in answer to an essay question. If you guess a letter – say "B" for a multiple-choice question – you may have guessed right. If you leave a blank as an answer to a multiple-choice question, the examiners may respect your feelings but it will not add a point to your score. Some exams may penalize you for wrong answers, so in such cases *only*, you may not want to guess unless you have some basis for your answer.

7) Suggestions
    a. Objective-type questions
        1. Examine the question booklet for proper sequence of pages and questions
        2. Read all instructions carefully
        3. Skip any question which seems too difficult; return to it after all other questions have been answered
        4. Apportion your time properly; do not spend too much time on any single question or group of questions

5. Note and underline key words – *all, most, fewest, least, best, worst, same, opposite*, etc.
6. Pay particular attention to negatives
7. Note unusual option, e.g., unduly long, short, complex, different or similar in content to the body of the question
8. Observe the use of "hedging" words – *probably, may, most likely*, etc.
9. Make sure that your answer is put next to the same number as the question
10. Do not second-guess unless you have good reason to believe the second answer is definitely more correct
11. Cross out original answer if you decide another answer is more accurate; do not erase until you are ready to hand your paper in
12. Answer all questions; guess unless instructed otherwise
13. Leave time for review

b. Essay questions
1. Read each question carefully
2. Determine exactly what is wanted. Underline key words or phrases.
3. Decide on outline or paragraph answer
4. Include many different points and elements unless asked to develop any one or two points or elements
5. Show impartiality by giving pros and cons unless directed to select one side only
6. Make and write down any assumptions you find necessary to answer the questions
7. Watch your English, grammar, punctuation and choice of words
8. Time your answers; don't crowd material

8) Answering the essay question

Most essay questions can be answered by framing the specific response around several key words or ideas. Here are a few such key words or ideas:

M's: manpower, materials, methods, money, management
P's: purpose, program, policy, plan, procedure, practice, problems, pitfalls, personnel, public relations

   a. Six basic steps in handling problems:
      1. Preliminary plan and background development
      2. Collect information, data and facts
      3. Analyze and interpret information, data and facts
      4. Analyze and develop solutions as well as make recommendations
      5. Prepare report and sell recommendations
      6. Install recommendations and follow up effectiveness

   b. Pitfalls to avoid
      1. *Taking things for granted* – A statement of the situation does not necessarily imply that each of the elements is necessarily true; for example, a complaint may be invalid and biased so that all that can be taken for granted is that a complaint has been registered

2. *Considering only one side of a situation* – Wherever possible, indicate several alternatives and then point out the reasons you selected the best one
3. *Failing to indicate follow up* – Whenever your answer indicates action on your part, make certain that you will take proper follow-up action to see how successful your recommendations, procedures or actions turn out to be
4. *Taking too long in answering any single question* – Remember to time your answers properly

IX. AFTER THE TEST

Scoring procedures differ in detail among civil service jurisdictions although the general principles are the same. Whether the papers are hand-scored or graded by machine we have described, they are nearly always graded by number. That is, the person who marks the paper knows only the number – never the name – of the applicant. Not until all the papers have been graded will they be matched with names. If other tests, such as training and experience or oral interview ratings have been given, scores will be combined. Different parts of the examination usually have different weights. For example, the written test might count 60 percent of the final grade, and a rating of training and experience 40 percent. In many jurisdictions, veterans will have a certain number of points added to their grades.

After the final grade has been determined, the names are placed in grade order and an eligible list is established. There are various methods for resolving ties between those who get the same final grade – probably the most common is to place first the name of the person whose application was received first. Job offers are made from the eligible list in the order the names appear on it. You will be notified of your grade and your rank as soon as all these computations have been made. This will be done as rapidly as possible.

People who are found to meet the requirements in the announcement are called "eligibles." Their names are put on a list of eligible candidates. An eligible's chances of getting a job depend on how high he stands on this list and how fast agencies are filling jobs from the list.

When a job is to be filled from a list of eligibles, the agency asks for the names of people on the list of eligibles for that job. When the civil service commission receives this request, it sends to the agency the names of the three people highest on this list. Or, if the job to be filled has specialized requirements, the office sends the agency the names of the top three persons who meet these requirements from the general list.

The appointing officer makes a choice from among the three people whose names were sent to him. If the selected person accepts the appointment, the names of the others are put back on the list to be considered for future openings.

That is the rule in hiring from all kinds of eligible lists, whether they are for typist, carpenter, chemist, or something else. For every vacancy, the appointing officer has his choice of any one of the top three eligibles on the list. This explains why the person whose name is on top of the list sometimes does not get an appointment when some of the persons lower on the list do. If the appointing officer chooses the second or third eligible, the No. 1 eligible does not get a job at once, but stays on the list until he is appointed or the list is terminated.

X. HOW TO PASS THE INTERVIEW TEST

The examination for which you applied requires an oral interview test. You have already taken the written test and you are now being called for the interview test – the final part of the formal examination.

You may think that it is not possible to prepare for an interview test and that there are no procedures to follow during an interview. Our purpose is to point out some things you can do in advance that will help you and some good rules to follow and pitfalls to avoid while you are being interviewed.

What is an interview supposed to test?

The written examination is designed to test the technical knowledge and competence of the candidate; the oral is designed to evaluate intangible qualities, not readily measured otherwise, and to establish a list showing the relative fitness of each candidate – as measured against his competitors – for the position sought. Scoring is not on the basis of "right" and "wrong," but on a sliding scale of values ranging from "not passable" to "outstanding." As a matter of fact, it is possible to achieve a relatively low score without a single "incorrect" answer because of evident weakness in the qualities being measured.

Occasionally, an examination may consist entirely of an oral test – either an individual or a group oral. In such cases, information is sought concerning the technical knowledges and abilities of the candidate, since there has been no written examination for this purpose. More commonly, however, an oral test is used to supplement a written examination.

Who conducts interviews?

The composition of oral boards varies among different jurisdictions. In nearly all, a representative of the personnel department serves as chairman. One of the members of the board may be a representative of the department in which the candidate would work. In some cases, "outside experts" are used, and, frequently, a businessman or some other representative of the general public is asked to serve. Labor and management or other special groups may be represented. The aim is to secure the services of experts in the appropriate field.

However the board is composed, it is a good idea (and not at all improper or unethical) to ascertain in advance of the interview who the members are and what groups they represent. When you are introduced to them, you will have some idea of their backgrounds and interests, and at least you will not stutter and stammer over their names.

What should be done before the interview?

While knowledge about the board members is useful and takes some of the surprise element out of the interview, there is other preparation which is more substantive. It *is* possible to prepare for an oral interview – in several ways:

1) Keep a copy of your application and review it carefully before the interview

This may be the only document before the oral board, and the starting point of the interview. Know what education and experience you have listed there, and the sequence and dates of all of it. Sometimes the board will ask you to review the highlights of your experience for them; you should not have to hem and haw doing it.

2) Study the class specification and the examination announcement

Usually, the oral board has one or both of these to guide them. The qualities, characteristics or knowledges required by the position sought are stated in these documents. They offer valuable clues as to the nature of the oral interview. For example, if the job involves supervisory responsibilities, the announcement will usually indicate that knowledge of modern supervisory methods and the qualifications of the candidate as a supervisor will be tested. If so, you can expect such questions, frequently in the form of a hypothetical situation which you are expected to solve. NEVER go into an oral without knowledge of the duties and responsibilities of the job you seek.

3) Think through each qualification required

Try to visualize the kind of questions you would ask if you were a board member. How well could you answer them? Try especially to appraise your own knowledge and background in each area, *measured against the job sought*, and identify any areas in which you are weak. Be critical and realistic – do not flatter yourself.

4) Do some general reading in areas in which you feel you may be weak

For example, if the job involves supervision and your past experience has NOT, some general reading in supervisory methods and practices, particularly in the field of human relations, might be useful. Do NOT study agency procedures or detailed manuals. The oral board will be testing your understanding and capacity, not your memory.

5) Get a good night's sleep and watch your general health and mental attitude

You will want a clear head at the interview. Take care of a cold or any other minor ailment, and of course, no hangovers.

What should be done on the day of the interview?

Now comes the day of the interview itself. Give yourself plenty of time to get there. Plan to arrive somewhat ahead of the scheduled time, particularly if your appointment is in the fore part of the day. If a previous candidate fails to appear, the board might be ready for you a bit early. By early afternoon an oral board is almost invariably behind schedule if there are many candidates, and you may have to wait. Take along a book or magazine to read, or your application to review, but leave any extraneous material in the waiting room when you go in for your interview. In any event, relax and compose yourself.

The matter of dress is important. The board is forming impressions about you – from your experience, your manners, your attitude, and your appearance. Give your personal appearance careful attention. Dress your best, but not your flashiest. Choose conservative, appropriate clothing, and be sure it is immaculate. This is a business interview, and your appearance should indicate that you regard it as such. Besides, being well groomed and properly dressed will help boost your confidence.

Sooner or later, someone will call your name and escort you into the interview room. *This is it.* From here on you are on your own. It is too late for any more preparation. But remember, you asked for this opportunity to prove your fitness, and you are here because your request was granted.

What happens when you go in?

The usual sequence of events will be as follows: The clerk (who is often the board stenographer) will introduce you to the chairman of the oral board, who will introduce you to the other members of the board. Acknowledge the introductions before you sit down. Do not be surprised if you find a microphone facing you or a stenotypist sitting by. Oral interviews are usually recorded in the event of an appeal or other review.

Usually the chairman of the board will open the interview by reviewing the highlights of your education and work experience from your application – primarily for the benefit of the other members of the board, as well as to get the material into the record. Do not interrupt or comment unless there is an error or significant misinterpretation; if that is the case, do not hesitate. But do not quibble about insignificant matters. Also, he will usually ask you some question about your education, experience or your present job – partly to get you to start talking and to establish the interviewing "rapport." He may start the actual questioning, or turn it over to one of the other members. Frequently, each member undertakes the questioning on a particular area, one in which he is perhaps most competent, so you can expect each member to participate in the examination. Because time is limited, you may also expect some rather abrupt switches in the direction the questioning takes, so do not be upset by it. Normally, a board member will not pursue a single line of questioning unless he discovers a particular strength or weakness.

After each member has participated, the chairman will usually ask whether any member has any further questions, then will ask you if you have anything you wish to add. Unless you are expecting this question, it may floor you. Worse, it may start you off on an extended, extemporaneous speech. The board is not usually seeking more information. The question is principally to offer you a last opportunity to present further qualifications or to indicate that you have nothing to add. So, if you feel that a significant qualification or characteristic has been overlooked, it is proper to point it out in a sentence or so. Do not compliment the board on the thoroughness of their examination – they have been sketchy, and you know it. If you wish, merely say, "No thank you, I have nothing further to add." This is a point where you can "talk yourself out" of a good impression or fail to present an important bit of information. Remember, *you close the interview yourself.*

The chairman will then say, "That is all, Mr. _____, thank you." Do not be startled; the interview is over, and quicker than you think. Thank him, gather your belongings and take your leave. Save your sigh of relief for the other side of the door.

How to put your best foot forward

Throughout this entire process, you may feel that the board individually and collectively is trying to pierce your defenses, seek out your hidden weaknesses and embarrass and confuse you. Actually, this is not true. They are obliged to make an appraisal of your qualifications for the job you are seeking, and they want to see you in your best light. Remember, they must interview all candidates and a non-cooperative candidate may become a failure in spite of their best efforts to bring out his qualifications. Here are 15 suggestions that will help you:

1) **Be natural – Keep your attitude confident, not cocky**

If you are not confident that you can do the job, do not expect the board to be. Do not apologize for your weaknesses, try to bring out your strong points. The board is interested in a positive, not negative, presentation. Cockiness will antagonize any board member and make him wonder if you are covering up a weakness by a false show of strength.

2) **Get comfortable, but don't lounge or sprawl**

Sit erectly but not stiffly. A careless posture may lead the board to conclude that you are careless in other things, or at least that you are not impressed by the importance of the occasion. Either conclusion is natural, even if incorrect. Do not fuss with your clothing, a pencil or an ashtray. Your hands may occasionally be useful to emphasize a point; do not let them become a point of distraction.

3) **Do not wisecrack or make small talk**

This is a serious situation, and your attitude should show that you consider it as such. Further, the time of the board is limited – they do not want to waste it, and neither should you.

4) Do not exaggerate your experience or abilities

In the first place, from information in the application or other interviews and sources, the board may know more about you than you think. Secondly, you probably will not get away with it. An experienced board is rather adept at spotting such a situation, so do not take the chance.

5) If you know a board member, do not make a point of it, yet do not hide it

Certainly you are not fooling him, and probably not the other members of the board. Do not try to take advantage of your acquaintanceship – it will probably do you little good.

6) Do not dominate the interview

Let the board do that. They will give you the clues – do not assume that you have to do all the talking. Realize that the board has a number of questions to ask you, and do not try to take up all the interview time by showing off your extensive knowledge of the answer to the first one.

7) Be attentive

You only have 20 minutes or so, and you should keep your attention at its sharpest throughout. When a member is addressing a problem or question to you, give him your undivided attention. Address your reply principally to him, but do not exclude the other board members.

8) Do not interrupt

A board member may be stating a problem for you to analyze. He will ask you a question when the time comes. Let him state the problem, and wait for the question.

9) Make sure you understand the question

Do not try to answer until you are sure what the question is. If it is not clear, restate it in your own words or ask the board member to clarify it for you. However, do not haggle about minor elements.

10) Reply promptly but not hastily

A common entry on oral board rating sheets is "candidate responded readily," or "candidate hesitated in replies." Respond as promptly and quickly as you can, but do not jump to a hasty, ill-considered answer.

11) Do not be peremptory in your answers

A brief answer is proper – but do not fire your answer back. That is a losing game from your point of view. The board member can probably ask questions much faster than you can answer them.

12) Do not try to create the answer you think the board member wants

He is interested in what kind of mind you have and how it works – not in playing games. Furthermore, he can usually spot this practice and will actually grade you down on it.

13) Do not switch sides in your reply merely to agree with a board member

Frequently, a member will take a contrary position merely to draw you out and to see if you are willing and able to defend your point of view. Do not start a debate, yet do not surrender a good position. If a position is worth taking, it is worth defending.

14) Do not be afraid to admit an error in judgment if you are shown to be wrong
The board knows that you are forced to reply without any opportunity for careful consideration. Your answer may be demonstrably wrong. If so, admit it and get on with the interview.

15) Do not dwell at length on your present job
The opening question may relate to your present assignment. Answer the question but do not go into an extended discussion. You are being examined for a *new* job, not your present one. As a matter of fact, try to phrase ALL your answers in terms of the job for which you are being examined.

Basis of Rating
Probably you will forget most of these "do's" and "don'ts" when you walk into the oral interview room. Even remembering them all will not ensure you a passing grade. Perhaps you did not have the qualifications in the first place. But remembering them will help you to put your best foot forward, without treading on the toes of the board members.

Rumor and popular opinion to the contrary notwithstanding, an oral board wants you to make the best appearance possible. They know you are under pressure – but they also want to see how you respond to it as a guide to what your reaction would be under the pressures of the job you seek. They will be influenced by the degree of poise you display, the personal traits you show and the manner in which you respond.

ABOUT THIS BOOK

This book contains tests divided into Examination Sections. Go through each test, answering every question in the margin. We have also attached a sample answer sheet at the back of the book that can be removed and used. At the end of each test look at the answer key and check your answers. On the ones you got wrong, look at the right answer choice and learn. Do not fill in the answers first. Do not memorize the questions and answers, but understand the answer and principles involved. On your test, the questions will likely be different from the samples. Questions are changed and new ones added. If you understand these past questions you should have success with any changes that arise. Tests may consist of several types of questions. We have additional books on each subject should more study be advisable or necessary for you. Finally, the more you study, the better prepared you will be. This book is intended to be the last thing you study before you walk into the examination room. Prior study of relevant texts is also recommended. NLC publishes some of these in our Fundamental Series. Knowledge and good sense are important factors in passing your exam. Good luck also helps. So now study this Passbook, absorb the material contained within and take that knowledge into the examination. Then do your best to pass that exam.

EXAMINATION SECTION

EXAMINATION SECTION
TEST 1

DIRECTIONS: Each question or incomplete statement is followed by several suggested answers or completions. Select the one that BEST answers the question or completes the statement. *PRINT THE LETTER OF THE CORRECT ANSWER IN THE SPACE AT THE RIGHT.*

1. The philosophy of case work is based upon the 1.____

    A. recognition of the dignity of the human person
    B. place of the agency in the community
    C. importance of planning realistically with clients
    D. role of the worker in case work treatment

2. Social case work aims CHIEFLY to 2.____

    A. give material assistance and help the client achieve success
    B. find the reasons for the person's difficulty and refer him for help to the proper source
    C. help the person through a professional relationship to gain a better understanding of his problem and to help him make a satisfactory adjustment
    D. improve the person's environment

3. The interview in case work is used CHIEFLY 3.____

    A. to get proof of data required in evaluating the client's problems and resources
    B. as a tool to explore with the client his feelings about his problem, as well as about the problem itself, so as to arrive at a plan of treatment
    C. because it is less expensive than other methods of work
    D. for statistical purposes on the basis of the worker's record

4. The case work relationship between the worker and the client is important CHIEFLY because it 4.____

    A. is a friendly relationship which the client needs at times
    B. provides an opportunity for the client to talk things out
    C. is a professional relationship to which the worker brings specific knowledge and skills to help another person
    D. provides concentrated attention to problems over a short period of time

5. The case worker, to be MOST effective in helping another person, must 5.____

    A. be free from prejudice of any kind
    B. have a wide knowledge of the individual's cultural background
    C. have received help himself in order to better understand the client's feelings
    D. be aware as much as possible about his own feelings regarding his client

6. One of the BEST known marks of the mature person is the ability to 6.____

    A. control his feelings in difficult situations
    B. defer future pleasures or gratifications for long-term goals
    C. take things as they come, trusting in luck
    D. enjoy a great many outside interests in life

7. An adult with a mental age of 9 years was regarded psychologically as

   A. of normal mentality
   B. a moron
   C. an imbecile
   D. an idiot

8. The one of the following conditions which bears NO causative relationship to mental deficiency is

   A. heredity
   B. cerebral defect
   C. early postnatal trauma
   D. dementia

9. Physical conditions which are caused by emotional conflicts are GENERALLY referred to as being

   A. psycho-social
   B. hypochondriacal
   C. psychosomatic
   D. psychotic

10. Of the following conditions, the one in which anxiety is NOT generally found is

    A. psychopathic personality
    B. mild hysteria
    C. psychoneurosis
    D. compulsive-obsessive personality

11. Kleptomania may BEST be described as a

    A. neurotic drive to accumulate personal property through compulsive acts in order to dispose of it to others with whom one wishes friendship
    B. type of neurosis which manifests itself in an uncontrollable impulse to steal without economic motivation
    C. psychopathic trait which is probably hereditary in nature
    D. manifestation of punishment-inviting behavior based upon guilt feelings for some other crime or wrongdoing, fantasied or real, committed as a child

12. The one of the following tests which is NOT ordinarily used as a projective technique is the

    A. Wechsler Bellevue Scale
    B. Rorschach Test
    C. Thematic Apperception Test
    D. Jung Free Association Test

13. An outstanding personality test in use at the present time is the Rorschach Test. Of the following considerations, the GREATEST value of this test to the psychiatrist and social worker is that it

    A. provides practical recommendations with reference to further educational and vocational training possibilities for the person tested
    B. reveals in quick, concise form the hereditary factors affecting the individual personality
    C. helps in substantiating a diagnosis of juvenile delinquency
    D. helps in a diagnostic formulation and in determining differential treatment

14. Of the following, the one through which ethical values are MOST generally acquired is   14.____

    A. heredity
    B. early training in school
    C. admonition and strict corrective measures by parents and other supervising adults
    D. integration into the self of parental values and attitudes

15. Records show that MOST crimes in the United States are committed by persons _____   15.____
    years of age.

    A. under 18   B. from 18 to 25
    C. from 30 to 40   D. above 40

16. According to current theories of criminology, the one of the following which is regarded as   16.____
    the MOST important cause of delinquency is

    A. personality maladjustment
    B. lack of proper housing
    C. mental deficiency
    D. community indifference to the need for recreational facilities

17. Delinquent behavior is MOST generally a result of   17.____

    A. living and growing up in an environment that is both socially and financially
       deprived
    B. a lack of educational opportunity for development of individual skills
    C. multiple factors - psychological, bio-social, emotional, and environmental
    D. low frustration tolerance of many parents toward problems of married life

18. Unmarried mothers USUALLY   18.____

    A. come from homes of poor economic status
    B. have had poor moral training in their youth
    C. are amoral or have little or no feeling of guilt
    D. all of the above

19. Alcoholism in the United States is USUALLY caused by   19.____

    A. the sense of frustration in one's work
    B. inadequacy of recreational facilities
    C. neurotic conflicts expressed in drinking excessively
    D. shyness and timidity

20. The MOST distinctive characteristic of the chronic alcoholic is that he drinks alcohol   20.____

    A. socially   B. compulsively
    C. periodically   D. secretly

21. *The chronic alcoholic is the person who cannot face reality without alcohol, and yet*   21.____
    whose adequate adjustment to reality is impossible so long as he uses alcohol.
    On the basis of this quotation, it is MOST reasonable to conclude that individuals over-
    indulge in alcohol because alcohol

A. deadens the sense of conflict, giving the individual an illusion of social competence and a feeling of well-being and success
B. provides the individual with an outlet to display his feelings of good-fellowship and cheerfulness which are characteristic of his extroverted personality
C. affords an escape technique from habitual irrational fears, but does not affect rational fears
D. offers an escape from imagery and feelings of superiority which cause tension and anxiety

22. The one of the following drugs to which a person is LEAST likely to become addicted is

    A. opium   B. morphine   C. marijuana   D. heroin

23. Teenagers who become addicted to the use of drugs are MOST generally

    A. mentally defective
    B. paranoid
    C. normally adventurous
    D. emotionally disturbed

24. In the light of the current high rate of addiction to drugs among youths throughout the country, the one of the following statements which is generally considered to be LEAST correct is that

    A. a relatively large number of children and youths who experiment with drugs become addicts
    B. youths who use narcotics do so because of some emotional and personality disturbance
    C. youthful addicts are found largely among those who suffer to an abnormal extent deprivations in their personal development and growth
    D. the great majority of youthful addicts have had unfortunate home experiences and practically no contact with established community agencies

25. The Social Service Exchange is utilized by probation officers PRIMARILY in order to

    A. facilitate the operation of the Interstate Compact for the transfer of probationers
    B. secure a complete criminal record of the defendant awaiting sentence
    C. secure a listing of agencies which have known the defendant or his family
    D. acquire a developmental history of the defendant

Questions 26-32.

DIRECTIONS: Column I lists terms and Column II gives definitions. For each term listed in Column I, select its definition from Column II, and write the letter which precedes this definition.

COLUMN I

26. acquittal

27. arrest

28. citation

29. commitment

30. indictment

31. recidivism

32. rendition

COLUMN II

A. surrender by one state of a person found in that state for prosecution in another state having jurisdiction to try the charge

B. an official summons or notice to a person to appear before a court

C. the act of taking a person into custody by authority of law

D. a formal written statement charging one or more persons with an offense as formulated by the prosecutor and found by a grand jury

E. bringing the accused before a court to answer a minimal charge

F. an accusation of any offense or unlawful state of affairs originating with a grand jury from their own knowledge or observation

G. consignment to a place of official confinement of a person found guilty of a crime

H. finding the accused not guilty of a crime after trial

I. agreement to appear in court upon request, with-out bond

J. reversion or relapse into prior criminal habits even after punishment

26.____
27.____
28.____
29.____
30.____
31.____
32.____

33. According to the statutes, a misdemeanor is an offense

    A. which is punishable by not more than an indeterminate term of from two to four years in a state prison
    B. not accompanied by physical violence
    C. for which reformatory sentence is mandatory unless sentence is suspended
    D. punishable by not more than one year of imprisonment

34. A person who is found guilty of a misdemeanor in a court may be kept under probationary supervision for

    A. a maximum of one year
    B. a period not to exceed one-half of the prison term prescribed by law
    C. a maximum of three years
    D. as long as the court desires

35. According to the State Griminal Procedure Law, the period of probation in the case of a child may NOT extend beyond

    A. his minority
    B. three years from the date of disposition
    C. the maximum time for which he might have been institutionalized
    D. the time required for him to make an adequate adjustment

36. According to the Criminal Procedure Law, the court which imposed the conditions of probation may

    A. not change them under any circumstances
    B. subsequently modify these conditions
    C. revise them only after one year of probation
    D. revise but not increase them

37. In cases of adult offenders, probation differs from parole in that probation involves

    A. suspension of sentence
    B. supervision after imprisonment
    C. supervision as a preliminary to parole
    D. un unlimited period of surveillance

38. One of the duties of the probation officer during pre-sentence investigations and the supervision process is the consideration of evidence.
    Of the following statements relating to the different types of evidence, the one which is LEAST accurate is that

    A. real evidence consists of any facts which are secured by first-hand experience
    B. testimonial evidence is the assertion of a human being
    C. hearsay evidence has little or no validity in probation practice
    D. expert evidence is the testimony of a person with specialized knowledge of or skill in a particular field

39. *The effect of rumors may be temporary or lasting. If they are reinforced and if there is no appreciable conflict with other and then with newer impulses, they are likely to persist. The rumor-engendered impression, moreover, is often the first reaction to an event. Subsequent information labors under a psychological handicap even when it is perceived. If a man is ruined by lies which people have the desire to believe, only compelling truths can resurrect him. The truths, though, will not be responded to eagerly, and they most probably will not drive out all the effects from the past.*
Of the following, the statement which is MOST accurate on the basis of the above paragraph is that

   A. rumor-engendered impressions are readily obliterated if disproved by compelling truths
   B. uninformed rumors should not be spread since they usually ruin people's lives
   C. false rumors are disproved with difficulty, and the first impression of uncontested and disproved false rumors is likely to continue
   D. unlike the normal reaction to the rumor proved false, there is a psychological handicap in accepting the uncontested rumor

40. Of the following, the MAIN reason for keeping a case record in probation or parole supervision is to

   A. present a verified picture of all legal aspects of the case
   B. provide a complete and objective understanding of the person through knowledge gained from relatives, friends, and other agencies
   C. improve the quality of service to the probationer and to help the probation officer to understand him and his situation
   D. give a realistic picture of the employment and recreational activities of the person in order to evaluate his progress toward rehabilitation

KEY (CORRECT ANSWERS)

1.	A	11.	B	21.	A	31.	J
2.	C	12.	A	22.	C	32.	A
3.	B	13.	D	23.	D	33.	D
4.	C	14.	D	24.	A	34.	C
5.	D	15.	B	25.	C	35.	A
6.	A	16.	A	26.	H	36.	B
7.	B	17.	C	27.	C	37.	A
8.	D	18.	D	28.	B	38.	C
9.	C	19.	C	29.	G	39.	C
10.	A	20.	B	30.	D	40.	C

TEST 2

DIRECTIONS: Each question or incomplete statement is followed by several suggested answers or completions. Select the one that BEST answers the question or completes the statement. *PRINT THE LETTER OF THE CORRECT ANSWER IN THE SPACE AT THE RIGHT.*

1. The MOST accurate of the following statements concerning probation case records is that they

   A. are generically different from those in use in the private case work field
   B. differ radically from the procedural records of the court
   C. should of necessity place less emphasis on the treatment than on the investigation of a person on probation
   D. should emphasize surveillance factors of probation

2. Of the following reasons for maintaining records in the probation department, the one which has the LEAST significance to the agency and the probation officer is that

   A. case recording is an essential adjunct to the practice of case work
   B. accurate and current case records facilitate treatment
   C. case records represent the agency's knowledge, insight, experience, efforts, and plans in individual situations
   D. case records represent evidence with which to deny false accusations and derogatory evaluative statements arising in the community

3. The method of case recording which reflects the interaction between the client and the social worker around the problem as the client sees it and feels about it is known as

   A. chronological
   B. process
   C. summary
   D. topical

4. The one of the following which is the MOST important asset for a probation officer is

   A. a well-integrated personality
   B. expert knowledge of crime causation
   C. comprehensive knowledge of community resources
   D. good health to enable the office to cope with the hazards of probation work

5. A probation officer, newly assigned as a worker in a legalistic agency structure, must set goals for himself as a learner in a new experience.
   The one of the following which MOST comprehensively and clearly states the learning goals of the new probation officer is to gain

   A. a comprehensive knowledge of the basic structure of the agency and the laws under which it operates
   B. a clear understanding of the objectives of the programs of the agency and of the underlying philosophy which governs the manner in which these programs are administered
   C. the integration of knowledge, development of skills in practice and growth in personal emotional structure necessary to enable him to help others most effectively
   D. the ability to recognize distress and signs of emotional disturbance in people and to treat symptomatic behavior while working within the agency framework

6. The one of the following statements which is LEAST accurate is:

   A. The type of evidence available in making a diagnosis of a person under investigation by a probation officer generally is not of a probative value equal to that of facts found in the exact sciences
   B. The rehabilitative treatment of a probationer lacks the precision used in treating physical diseases
   C. The vast background of experience in probation work today makes it possible for the probation officer to diagnose with certainty the personality and character of the probationer
   D. In considering evidence during an investigation, the probation officer can never be sure whether some fact has been overlooked that might alter the entire analysis

7. The MOST accurate of the following statements with respect to reciprocal state legislation to compel the support of dependent wives and children, better known as the Uniform Support of Dependents Law, is:

   A. The amount of support allotted to women and children has been made uniform throughout the United States
   B. Provision has been made for the deserted wife to make the complaint in the state of residence and for the order of support against her husband to be made in the state where her husband now resides
   C. Sufficient federal funds have been provided to make it possible for the deserted wife to travel to the state where the deserting husband has been located and there make the proper complaint for support
   D. The legal requirements of extradition concerning deserting husbands have been eased, thereby facilitating their return to the state where the spouse resides to face appropriate criminal action

8. The one of the following statements which contains the basic principle upon which *Aggressive Case Work* GENERALLY operates is:

   A. When a client applies for help with a delinquent child, the worker, following a complete study of the problem, forcefully and very definitely defines the solution of the problem to the client
   B. The social worker waits until the neglect of a child by his parents reaches a point where the court should take action and then proceeds to remove the child from his home
   C. New social work techniques are used to arouse the client's interest so that he voluntarily requests aid
   D. The social worker goes out to meet the client in his own setting

9. Treatment of the delinquent child must be based on the child's individual needs PRIMARILY because

   A. the child's needs are usually for adequate recreational facilities and better home conditions
   B. social treatment depends upon social diagnosis, and sound diagnosis requires knowledge of the person
   C. behavior is usually determined by environment, which is unique for each person
   D. the child's needs are usually less complicated than those of an adult

10. It has been said that the probation officer working with a delinquent child *becomes for the child the symbol of the authority against which he rebels.* The task of the probation officer is to convert what appears to be a handicap into an asset.
    Of the following approaches to this problem, the one which serves the probation officer MOST advantageously is to

    A. disguise his role of authority by becoming a friend to the child, who will then respond in a more personal way by talking freely about himself and his experiences
    B. strengthen the parents so that they will relax their parental authoritative role and be more permissive in their discipline of the child
    C. maintain his authority while offering guidance and counsel on the basis of disciplined concern for the child, genuine warmth, and willingness and capacity to enter into his feelings and thinking about persons, situations, and things
    D. refer the case to an agency in the community where the non-authoritative setting will permit reaching the child on a social and psychological basis through the use of treatment techniques for emotionally disturbed children

11. Of the following statements relating to probation of known alcoholics, the one which is MOST accurate is:

    A. In order to help an alcoholic person under supervision, a probation officer should consider it important for the family to understand something of the probationer's problem
    B. Referral of alcoholic probationers to medical facilities for the administration of certain drugs has proven successful in practically all cases
    C. Research to date demonstrates that, in general, alcoholics on probation make an easy and adequate adjustment
    D. Most domestic relations problems are caused by alcoholics or heavy drinkers

12. Probation officers frequently encounter problems of young adults, either single or married, with deep, unresolved dependency conflicts who cannot make mature adjustments in their work, living arrangements, or handling of their marital and parent-child relationships. The one of the following which is MOST appropriate in case work with individuals or families presenting problems of this type is

    A. environment service, affording immediate adjustments of an external character
    B. specific advice and concrete suggestions given directly by the case worker upon his own initiative
    C. case work treatment through which the person learns to handle his situation realistically with lessened anxiety as a result of a clearer understanding of deep-seated, repressed emotional material
    D. supportive counseling in helping the person to gain some beginning insight into his basic problem so that he can be helped, if need is indicated, to move on to psychiatric treatment

13. In supervising an unemployed probationer, the one of the following actions which ordinarily represents GOOD probation practice is to

    A. refer the probationer immediately to the State Unemployment Bureau
    B. encourage the probationer and give him supportive help in using his own initiative to secure employment

C. refer the probationer to personal employer contacts known to the probation officer
D. fix a time limit for the probationer to get a job before returning him to court for violation of probation

14. The majority of cases coming to a court because of marital discord are presented at a time of crisis.
Of the following approaches, the one which is MOST essential to the probation officer in offering help to a family in this situation is

   A. early analysis of his own attitudes and reactions in differentiating between factors already present in the personalities of the husband and wife and of situational factors
   B. immediate determination of the legal aspects of the marriage problem and recognition and handling of transference and counter-transference in the case work relationship
   C. establishing of a relationship which will enable the client to express his feelings and to present the problem as he sees it, thus enabling the probation officer to arrive at a sound diagnostic judgment
   D. offering of a relationship at a level that will provide a vent to the husband and wife, endeavoring to use psychological support to direct them towards reconciliation

15. Mr. X, while on probation on a charge of desertion, again absconds, leaving his family without provision for support. The one of the following actions to be taken FIRST by the probation officer in apprehending the probationer is to

   A. file a probation warrant with the local police department
   B. prepare a violation of probation report requesting the court to issue a bench warrant
   C. request the court to revoke the man's probation and advise his wife to immediately make a new complaint of desertion
   D. interview the deserted wife in order to understand her feelings about her husband's desertion and to discuss with her, if she wishes, the possible whereabouts of the probationer

16. A boy of 15, on probation for one year in the Children's Court on an original petition of delinquency made by his inadequate mother, has shown no improvement in his behavior, is beyond her control, and is associating with a gang consisting of other seriously delinquent boys.
Of the following courses of action, the one which is MOST advisable for the probation officer to pursue is to

   A. refer the boy for psychiatric evaluation or recommendation to determine whether he should be committed to an institution where he might receive treatment in a controlled environment
   B. refer the family to a social agency for counseling to improve the home situation
   C. arrange to have more frequent interviews with the mother
   D. caution the boy that unless he improves his behavior and disassociates himself from the gang, the probation officer will be forced to recommend commitment to an institution

5 (#2)

17. An adolescent girl held as a material witness in a case of rape expresses strong hostility towards her mother, whom she claims always favored her younger brother. The mother says, in an interview, that she was always devoted to her own mother, now deceased, but that she was never able to confide in her or feel that she was understood by her. This knowledge of the mother's earlier experiences may provide a clue to the probation officer in understanding causative factors in the girl's behavior.
Of the following explanations, the one which MOST likely accounts for the poor relationship between mother and daughter is that the

   A. mother's greater interest in and warmth for her son would indicate that she had a better relationship with her own father than with her mother
   B. mother of the girl had lacked a warm, trusting relationship with her own mother and, therefore, provided an overpermissive atmosphere in her home for her daughter, believing that this would create a closer relationship between them
   C. girl's behavior springs from a fantasied maturity which is a spurious and unreal assumption of an adult status, often a temporary phase in adolescent growth
   D. mother of the girl probably had not worked through problems in relationship with her own mother and was unable, therefore, to establish a sound relationship with her daughter

17._____

18. A girl of 19, adjudicated as a wayward minor and placed on probation, is discovered by the probation officer to be a prostitute, although this has not yet come to the attention of the authorities.
The one of the following courses of action which is MOST advisable for the probation officer to pursue in these circumstances is to

   A. recommend that probation be revoked and that the girl be committed to an institution
   B. advise the girl that unless she discontinues this behavior the probation officer will have to report it to the court
   C. give the girl an opportunity to work out the problem for herself
   D. re-evaluate the case, discussing the matter with the probation officer's supervisor and determining appropriate action to take for the best interests of the community and the probationer

18._____

19. Mrs. A comes to a social agency asking for help with her 8-year-old son who is a truant from school and is generally willful and disobedient. Mr. A travels a good deal and is seldom at home. He has had very little part in the rearing of the child.
Of the following actions, the one which the case worker should take FIRST is to

   A. see the child in order to learn from him why he is misbehaving
   B. arrange to see the father in order to advise him to change his job
   C. explore with Mr. A her feelings about the child as well as her feelings about her husband's part in the family picture
   D. visit the school to discover the cause of the difficulty there

19._____

20. A 17-year-old male on probation in the Family Court tells his probation officer that he resents reporting to him because he was innocent of the crime for which he was placed on probation. In addition, he states he dislikes the probation officer.
In this situation, the one of the following courses of action which the probation officer should pursue is to

20._____

A. encourage the probationer to seek legal assistance to reopen the case
B. adopt a firm attitude indicating that he is not interested in the probationer's guilt or innocence and insisting that he comply with the probation conditions
C. seek to understand the reasons why the probationer dislikes him, at the same time indicating to him that he is free to explore legal assistance regarding his original offense
D. consider the probationer as rebellious and a potential community threat, recommending that probation be revoked

21. *A person's behavior is both shaped and judged by the expectations he and his culture have invested in his status and the major social roles he carries.*
According to this principle, a caseworker can BEST make effective professional judgments and plan proper treatment if he recognizes that

    A. the client's problem may stem from role conflicts
    B. the client faces difficulties serenely once he knows what society expects of him
    C. cultural values have little to do with a client's status
    D. the status-seeking individual is not able to comprehend the function of cultural values in his life

22. The diagnostic approach in social casework, often called the Freudian School, has as its basic premise the

    A. investigation of past events of the client's life experiences and functioning in order to understand his present situation
    B. study of the subconscious mind of the client as to his present attitude and understanding about his situation
    C. examination of behavioral motivation of the client
    D. solution of the client's problem through aptitude testing and group therapy

23. There is implicit in casework an acceptance of a client's value system which may be different from that of the caseworker.
Of the following, the MOST valid conclusion to be derived from this statement is that

    A. clients do not have moral standards
    B. the caseworkers' standards are always stricter than the clients' standards
    C. cultural patterns have little effect on value systems by either clients or caseworkers
    D. a caseworker has no right to insist on conformity of a client's behavior with his own standards

24. The establishment and maintenance of a professional relationship with a client is stressed in casework. This relationship should be

    A. clear, business-like, and delimited by the agency function
    B. permissive, friendly, and kindly, with the pace determined by the client
    C. warm, enabling, and consciously controlled by the caseworker
    D. variable and unpredictable because of the fluctuations in client need

25. There is great interest being shown currently in the possible merger of the child welfare and family casework fields, in private as well as public agencies.
The BEST argument in support of such a merger is that

A. families with child care problems would not be broken up through placement of children
B. the taxpayer's and the voluntary contributor's money would be saved
C. through intensive work with children, prevention of the development of behavior problems would be possible
D. new techniques in family casework treatment and the development of new community resources would probably result

26. Family casework involves working with parents and children about problems involving maintenance and survival.
Of the following types of problems, the MOST important one that a family caseworker has to handle generally involves

   A. relationships between siblings
   B. budgeting
   C. psychotherapeutic problems
   D. environmental deficiencies

27. The authoritative approach in casework, also known as aggressive casework, essentially involves

   A. the breakup of families whose members no longer get along together
   B. purposeful, persistent casework methods observing respect for the individual
   C. direct supervision of a family until their problems are resolved
   D. the application of techniques evolved by law enforcement agencies to social casework

28. The term ambivalence, as used in social casework, might BEST be illustrated by the

   A. inability of the client to follow the recommendations of the caseworker, due to his own unresolved conflicts
   B. presentation to the client of more than one reasonable course of action for the client to follow
   C. client's lack of any knowledge of how to solve his problem
   D. client's fears for his future welfare

29. There is general agreement among experts in the field that, when dealing with a client or handling a case, a caseworker should

   A. place emphasis on the objective aspects, directing her work primarily to the physical factors in the client that indicate need for change
   B. place emphasis on the environmental factors, especially those surrounding the client which have caused him to be in his present state
   C. give attention not only to the environmental factors and social experiences, but also the client's feelings about, and reactions to, his experience
   D. consider each factor in the case as a separate unit after carefully distinguishing between the truly environmental and the truly emotional factors

30. In casework practice, the unit of attention is generally considered to be the family, although in some agencies the client or patient is often viewed as being outside of his family.
The trend in modern casework with respect to the family of a client is to

A. involve the family wherever feasible in the total casework process
B. scientifically determine wherein the family is harmful to the client and try to make plans for the client to leave his family
C. educate the public so that families of clients will not interfere with agency plans
D. refer every member of the family for casework help

31. John L., 15, was referred to a youth counseling agency by the principal of the high school he attends because he has been truanting for the past six months. He is of above average intelligence, is in his sophomore year, and is currently failing 4 out of 5 of his courses. His mother says that he frequently comes home after midnight and is friendly with two boys with court records. The family group consists of John and his mother, who supports them by working as a secretary. The sisters, 19 and 21, are married and out of the home. Mr. L. deserted when John was 3. The principal told John he had to go to the youth counseling agency or be brought into court by the truant officer.
In beginning to work with John, the caseworker should FIRST

   A. recognize that since John did not come voluntarily, he will refuse casework treatment
   B. establish himself as an adult who will keep John in line
   C. secure more facts about John and his situation in order to determine further case activity
   D. promise that the agency will keep John from being sent to juvenile court

31._____

32. A client tells the social worker that he is planning to leave his job as a junior executive trainee in a department store for a job as a laborer which will pay him a higher salary. After exploring the client's reasons for making this move, the caseworker feels the plan is unwise since the trainee position offers a considerably better future.
In this situation, it would be BEST for the caseworker to

   A. attempt to dissuade the client from making the job change, pointing out the reasons for the inadvisability of the move
   B. allow the client to change jobs, without attempting to dissuade or counsel him
   C. refuse to give the client permission to change jobs, without an attempt to dissuade or counsel him
   D. try to dissuade the client from making the job change without giving the real reasons for thinking the move undesirable

32._____

33. Casework interviewing is always directed to the client and his situation.
The one of the following which is the MOST accurate statement with respect to the proper focus of an interview is that the

   A. caseworker limits the client to concentration on objective data
   B. client is generally permitted to talk about facts and feelings with no direction from the caseworker
   C. main focus in casework interviews is on feelings rather than facts
   D. caseworker is responsible for helping the client focus on any material which seems to be related to his problems or difficulties

33._____

34. A recent development in casework interviewing procedure, known as multiple-client interviewing, consists of interviews of the entire family at the same time. However, this may not be an effective casework method in certain situations.
Of the following, the situation in which the standard individual interview would be PREFERABLE is when

   A. family members derive consistent and major gratification from assisting each other in their destructive responses
   B. there is a crucial family conflict to which the members are reacting
   C. the family is overwhelmed by interpersonal anxieties which have not been explored
   D. the worker wants to determine the pattern of family interaction to further his diagnostic understanding

35. The one of the following which is the CHIEF value of verbatim recording of all or a portion of an important interview is the possibility it offers for

   A. careful study and clarification of psychological goals in treatment
   B. a prompt solution to the problem by preservation, in an orderly and concise fashion, of the full psychological and economic picture of the client's situation
   C. quick determination of the more obvious social goals and offering of concrete services by presentation of the essential facts
   D. supervision of experienced workers by showing the emotional overtones, subtle reactions, and intricate worker-client interchanges

36. Experts in the field of social casework recording generally agree that the kind of case material for which the narrative form of recording is MOST suitable is

   A. material that deals with feelings, attitudes, and client-worker relationships because this style permits the use of primary evidence in the form of verbal material and behavior observed in the interview
   B. social data, including eligibility material and family background history, because it can then be presented in a chronological, orderly fashion to enable the worker to select the desired facts
   C. personal facts concerning the individual's personality patterns and their growth and development because they can be seen in an orderly progression from primal immaturity until their ultimate stage of completion
   D. selectively chosen and documented material essential to a quicker and clearer understanding of the various ramifications of the case by a new worker, when responsibility for handling the client is reassigned

37. A case record includes relevant social and psychological facts about the client, the nature of his request, his feeling about his situation, his attitude towards the agency, and his use of and reaction to treatment.
In addition, it should ALWAYS contain

   A. routine history
   B. complete details of personality development and emotional relationships
   C. detailed process accounts of all contacts
   D. data necessary for understanding the problem and the factors important in arriving at a solution

38. The CHIEF basis for the inability of a troubled client to express his problem clearly to the caseworker is that the client

   A. sees his problem in complex terms and does not think it possible to give the caseworker the whole picture
   B. has erected defenses against emotions that seem to him inadmissible or intolerable
   C. cannot describe how he feels about his problem
   D. views the situation as unlikely to be solved and is blocked in self-expression

39. During his pre-sentence investigation, a defendant gave information about his participation in the offense which conflicted with the official version. He was placed on probation. Now the district attorney wishes to use him as a witness against a co-defendant and asks for permission to use the pre-sentence report as a basis for cross-examination.
    Of the following, the BEST course of action to take is to

   A. refuse to turn over the report on the ground that the report is the property of the court and its contents cannot be revealed without authority of the court
   B. turn over the report to the district attorney but caution him to hold the source of his information confidential
   C. refer the request to the Director of Probation on the ground that this involves policy which no one else is ever authorized to handle
   D. advise the district attorney's office that the entire report cannot be sent to him but portions of it may be discussed with his representative

40. During the course of a pre-sentence investigation, the defendant reveals certain details of the offense not previously known and involves others who have not been apprehended.
    Of the following, the FIRST action to be taken by the probation officer on the case is to

   A. discuss the matter with the chief probation officer, asking guidance on methods of procedure
   B. report the new information to the district attorney's office immediately
   C. withhold the information until it can be disclosed to the court through the pre-sentence report in order to let the court decide how it is to be used
   D. advise the client of the importance of this information and ask him if he is prepared to make the same disclosures to the district attorney

41. A young man on probation after an offense involving fraudulent checks and impersonation of an officer is given work at a hospital as an attendant. Within three weeks, he marries a nurse's aide. A full investigation discloses that he told her he was wealthy, of good family, working humbly to *prove* himself.
    Of the following, the FIRST action for the probation officer to take in this case is to

   A. secure a warrant and cause his arrest immediately
   B. check with the hospital to get other details
   C. attempt to analyze the behavior pattern for causative factors
   D. recommend that the young couple get an annulment

42. The wife of a former probationer telephones the probation office stating that her husband has disappeared and she is anxious to secure all possible leads in order to aid the police in looking for him.
    Of the following, the BEST reply to be made to her is that

A. this is a job for the police, but if there are any developments, she will be informed
B. the case is closed and no help can be given her
C. she should consult her religious advisor and her attorney
D. the husband has had numerous previous girlfriends to whom he might have returned

43. A person of foreign birth is placed on probation but understands little English and cannot read or write. Of the following, the MOST appropriate action is to

A. order him to attend night classes in English
B. direct him to obtain someone who speaks his language to interpret the condition of probation
C. encourage him to seek language training and tell him that his probation will be revoked if he shows unwillingness to overcome his language handicap
D. give him guidance in finding a language class which will fit his needs and situation

44. The probation officer who made the pre-sentence investigation on a certain case happens to be personally acquainted with the judge who imposed sentence. Some time later, the judge receives a letter from the sentenced prisoner. The judge asks the probation officer to investigate this letter and make a recommendation.
Of the following, the BEST action for the probation officer to take is to

A. make the investigation and report directly to the judge
B. ask the judge to speak to his superior about this assignment
C. complete the report and submit it to his superior for approval without prior consultation with the latter
D. report to his superior that he has had a request for a supplementary investigation and await his decision as to whether it should be assigned to him or another officer

45. Having read another agency's record for information, it is GOOD case reporting practice to

A. quote the agency worker as the source of information and include any pertinent opinions given in the agency file
B. identify the source and report it over your signature as a part of the record
C. use the words *it is alleged* or *according to a reliable source* or *we have been informed*
D. refer to the other agency as Confidential Source No. 1, etc.

46. The type of pre-sentence report which is of GREATEST value is one which contains

A. a diagnostic interpretation of the etiology of the offense
B. the essential facts and indicates the treatment needs of the defendant
C. the essential facts about the defendant
D. a supplemental psychiatric study

47. The LEAST important reason for a probation officer to make a pre-sentence investigation and report is to

A. assist the judge in making proper disposition of the case
B. find conditions within the family which need the services of other agencies

C. assist the probation officer who will supervise the defendant if he is placed on probation
D. provide a case record for the institution if the defendant is committed

48. The one of the following statements which is MOST accurate in regard to violation of probation is that a violator should be returned to court

    A. only if he is guilty of a serious violation
    B. if further use of the authority of the court will have a therapeutic value in the case
    C. only if his detention is necessary for community production
    D. if commitment to a correctional institution had been under consideration before he was placed on probation

49. In dealing with violations of probation which have resulted in arrest, the probation officer should FIRST

    A. arrange for an immediate hearing before the sentencing judge in the original case
    B. discuss and evaluate the new violation with the arresting officer
    C. place a detainer against the probationer
    D. secure a voluntary statement from the probationer, including mention of his guilt or innocence

50. A probation officer sees a man on the street whom he believes is being sought under warrant as a probation violator. The probationer is not under his supervision. Of the following, the FIRST action the probation officer should take is to

    A. identify himself to the man and attempt to determine the latter's identity
    B. warn the probationer and report to his office that he has seen the violator
    C. advise the probationer to give himself up
    D. immediately contact the probation officer who has been supervising this probationer

KEY (CORRECT ANSWERS)

1. B	11. A	21. A	31. C	41. C
2. D	12. D	22. A	32. A	42. A
3. B	13. B	23. D	33. D	43. D
4. A	14. C	24. C	34. A	44. D
5. C	15. D	25. D	35. A	45. B
6. C	16. A	26. D	36. A	46. B
7. B	17. D	27. B	37. D	47. B
8. D	18. D	28. A	38. B	48. B
9. B	19. C	29. C	39. A	49. B
10. C	20. C	30. A	40. D	50. A

EXAMINATION SECTION
TEST 1

DIRECTIONS: Each question or incomplete statement is followed by several suggested answers or completions. Select the one that BEST answers the question or completes the statement. *PRINT THE LETTER OF THE CORRECT ANSWER IN THE SPACE AT THE RIGHT.*

1. One of the earliest of the names associated with the probation movement is

   A. Homer Folks
   B. Ben Lindsey
   C. Helen D. Pigeon
   D. John Augustus

2. Of the following, the fundamental theory of probation rests MOST NEARLY on

   A. the fear of punishment
   B. exercise by the court of its power of compulsion
   C. a promise by the offender to better his ways
   D. the frequency of recidivism

3. Release of offenders under supervision as an alternative to punishment was FIRST developed as a legal system in

   A. Ancient Rome
   B. France
   C. the United States
   D. Great Britain

4. The social agency conducting an institution for the care and treatment of delinquent and emotionally disturbed boys, which was founded originally for the care of Black children only, is the

   A. Wiltwyck School
   B. Vanderbilt Clinic
   C. Craig Colony
   D. Claremont House

5. A probation officer encountering a reference to *prognosis* in a case report would MOST accurately associate the term with

   A. a casual relationship
   B. psychosis
   C. a congenital disease
   D. a forecast

6. A probation report which describes a youngster as perspicacious seeks to convey the impression to the reader that the youngster is

   A. loquacious
   B. clever
   C. shrewish
   D. garrulous

7. In reporting on a person who thinks he sees objects which are NOT present and may NOT be real, the probation officer should describe such an individual as having

   A. claustrophobia
   B. delusions
   C. hallucinations
   D. paranoia

8. A good probation report should possess some of the following qualities, the LEAST desirable of which is

   A. legibility
   B. clarity
   C. coherence
   D. invalidity

21

9. When interviewing an individual with a reputation for being a conciliatory person, the probation officer should MOST reasonably expect to find that he

   A. is flippantly smooth
   B. has an appeasing manner
   C. is fickle
   D. has an uncontrollable temper

10. A juvenile whose veracity is frequently doubted is BEST described as

    A. a fabricator
    B. an alien
    C. born out of wedlock
    D. underprivileged

11. An adolescent who is habitually discontented could BEST be described as

    A. invidious
    B. plaintive
    C. quibbling
    D. captious

12. Siblings are MOST easily identified by

    A. blood
    B. adoption proceedings
    C. color
    D. speech

13. Occupational therapy is MOST closely associated with

    A. vocational guidance
    B. position classification
    C. curative handicraft
    D. diathermic treatment

14. Of the following degrees of deviation from normal mentality, the one indicating the LEAST intelligence is the

    A. moron
    B. imbecile
    C. idiot
    D. borderline

15. The person whose duty it is to manage the estate of a minor or of an incompetent is called the

    A. executor
    B. probate officer
    C. amicus curiae
    D. guardian

16. An order for a witness to appear in court is called

    A. a subpoena
    B. an injunction
    C. a mandamus
    D. res judicata

17. *Ostensibly a sane person, yet severely mentally ill and dangerous to himself and others* is a description MOST commonly applied to a

    A. psychopath
    B. paraplegic
    C. paretic
    D. paranoid

18. The impact upon society of mental disease is MOST adequately indicated by

    A. its responsibility for sex crimes and delinquency
    B. the phenomenal growth of feeble-mindedness in the United States
    C. the increasing number of deaths resulting from it
    D. the burden of its disabling effects on the community

19. A deficiency disease is a disorder caused by a(n) 19.____

    A. deficiency of medical aid
    B. diet lacking certain vitamins or minerals
    C. lack of proper rest and relaxation
    D. insufficient quantity of sugar in the diet

20. Delinquency on the part of a child is believed to result PRIMARILY from 20.____

    A. emotional and personality maladjustments
    B. environmental handicaps
    C. physical disability
    D. sociological factors

21. In determining whether or not an offender should be placed on probation, the MOST important factor for the probation officer to consider is the 21.____

    A. attitude of the community
    B. personality of the offender
    C. offense
    D. attitude of the court

22. A probation officer who has an objective attitude in social research would 22.____

    A. deal only with concrete reality rather than with abstract ideas
    B. use only evidence favorable to the objective
    C. object to all new hypotheses
    D. follow the evidence regardless of personal interests

23. In collecting social evidence from personnel in the public school system of the city, a probation officer would expect to find that the one of the following who makes the BEST social witness is the 23.____

    A. principal of the school at which the offender was a pupil
    B. superintendent of schools
    C. teacher who is able to individualize his pupils
    D. truant officer

24. The BEST of the following reporting techniques in releasing statistical data of a social nature is to publish 24.____

    A. percentage figures
    B. ratio figures
    C. absolute figures
    D. a descriptive summary without such figures

25. Progressively minded probation officers agree that the type of social treatment given a delinquent should be determined PRIMARILY by the 25.____

    A. nature of the offense committed
    B. type and variety of social problems causing the delinquency
    C. size of the probation officer's case load
    D. plan recommended by the judge

26. From a psychological point of view, delinquency can MOST accurately be considered as

   A. a definite congenital trait which causes inability to adjust to society
   B. overt acts which come into conflict with natural instincts
   C. a symptom of a deeper maladjustment which manifests itself in an inability to adjust to society
   D. none of the above

27. The TRUE extent of delinquency and crime in the United States is

   A. known accurately on an annual basis
   B. estimated on an annual basis
   C. known accurately in certain fields
   D. gathered statistically during each census year

28. The belief that crime can be prevented BEST by enforcing laws rigidly is based on the theory that

   A. persons cannot continue criminal careers as freely during periods of incarceration
   B. suppression leads to sublimation
   C. punishment is the most effective deterrent known against lawbreakers
   D. multiplicity of laws causes confusion in their attempted enforcement

29. Studies of penology reveal that punishment has

   A. seldom served as a crime deterrent
   B. successfully served as a crime deterrent
   C. served as a crime deterrent only in cases of larceny
   D. not served as a crime deterrent because the penalties inflicted have been too moderate

30. In the classifications of crime listed below, the one in which the probation officer would expect to find the HIGHEST proportion of arrests of females would be recorded in uniform crime reports under the heading of

   A. assault   B. automobile theft
   C. burglary   D. rape

31. A national magazine conducting a long-term feature devoted to techniques of crime prevention regularly prints contributions from such persons as an ex-president of the United States, a mayor, a congressman, a governor, and a civil court judge.
   A probation officer would MOST logically conclude from this example that

   A. there is as yet a great deal of inconclusive thinking on the causes of crime and the treatment of those causes
   B. public officials are better judges of the effectiveness of crime prevention techniques than persons not in the public service
   C. the experiences of sociologists and psychiatrists have been wholly negative in the field of crime prevention
   D. the best approach to crime prevention is that which encompasses the activities of local, state, and federal officials of every type

32. The PRIMARY reason for recording the results of a probation investigation is that the

    A. law requires that this be done
    B. written record is more impressive and credible than an oral report
    C. reader exerts a minimum of effort in comprehending and digesting the information
    D. data obtained may be made secretly and permanently available

33. According to studies conducted on methods of questioning during intake procedure by interviewers such as probation officers, a truthful statement of fact is LEAST easily obtained from the person being questioned if he is

    A. allowed to use an uninterrupted narrative form of expression
    B. cross-examined frequently by the person doing the interviewing
    C. encouraged to present his facts in chronological order
    D. interrupted as seldom as possible

34. The CHIEF concern of the pre-sentence investigation in a criminal court should be, according to the views expressed by the most noted researchers in the field of probation, to

    A. speed up the court procedures so that more cases can be handled expeditiously
    B. discover the immediate cause of the offender's being brought before the court
    C. determine whether the person brought before the court is innocent or guilty of the charges lodged against him
    D. explore all the social factors that have a bearing on the personality and behavior of the offender

35. To a probation officer, the ultimate object of a pre-sentence investigation is

    A. knowledge that will insure the punishment of the offender if a crime has been committed
    B. knowledge that will protect society from the criminal
    C. understanding of the offender from the point of view of his possible re-integration as a self-sufficient and permanently useful member of society
    D. understanding of the offender that will explain why he committed the crime and will enable society to guard against that sort of criminal activity

36. Case study procedure differs from statistical procedure MOST markedly in that

    A. the basis for statistical study is observation
    B. statistical procedure can be divided into inventory, analysis, and inference
    C. incorrect data in statistical procedure may result in an incomplete analysis
    D. statistical procedure has a broad numerical base making restriction of subjects necessary

37. Suppose that a good probation department were identified by each of the features listed below.
    If you, a probation officer, were studying the organization of such an agency, you would expect to find its correctional program LEAST affected by the removal of its

    A. enlightened policies
    B. trained and competent personnel
    C. suitable equipment and supplies with which to have its work done
    D. advisory board of the most notable penologists in the country

38. The one of the following which BEST expresses one of the fundamental foundations of the probation system is a(n)

    A. desire to reward the first offender in order to encourage good conduct
    B. desire to protect society by facilitating the readjustment of the probationer
    C. economy measure designed to save the government the cost of supporting prisoners in institutions
    D. growing attitude of leniency toward offenders

39. From the point of view of the probation officer, to integrate into normal groups children presenting symptoms of mild behavior disorder would be

    A. too radical a proposal; it has never been tried successfully
    B. impracticable; participation of problem children would jeopardize the program of the other children in the group
    C. undesirable; children otherwise emotionally stable would tend to become corrupted
    D. beneficial; it would expose the problem children to the beneficent effect of group activity with children possessing conforming behavior patterns

40. The detention of children waiting for a court decision as to whether they should be retained on a charge of having committed a minor offense is considered socially undesirable by progressively minded probation officers because the

    A. children may be cleared of the charge and, therefore, found to have been detained without cause
    B. children may be subjected to emotional damage
    C. parents may become unnecessarily concerned over the children's absence from home
    D. community is charged with the expense of lodging and feeding the children

41. Of the PRIMARY functions of a modern police department in dealing with juvenile delinquency, one should be to

    A. arrest the parents of delinquents and hold them responsible for neglecting their duties as parents
    B. perform social case work with the families of delinquent children
    C. recommend the level of treatment for children presenting behavior problems
    D. take an active part in programs designed to prevent juvenile delinquency

42. Legally, the BEST definition of juvenile delinquency is: Any child under

    A. 18 who has deserted his home and who habitually associates with dissolute, vicious, or immoral persons
    B. 16 who has violated a city ordinance or who has committed any offense, except murder or manslaughter, against the laws of the state
    C. 18 who has violated a city ordinance or who has committed any offense, except murder or manslaughter, against the laws of the state
    D. 16 who is habitually disobedient to the reasonable and lawful commands of his parents and who habitually absents himself from school or who persistently violates school regulations

43. Current interest in child guidance clinics was developed because of an increasing belief 43.____
that

   A. at least one-tenth of the nation's youth is destined to end in prison if not given systematic guidance
   B. children should be treated as miniature adults
   C. many of the emotional and mental disabilities of later life result from unfortunate childhood experiences
   D. the best interests of the nation require standardization of each child's education

44. A probationary sentence, such as the one given Joseph Buttafuoco for statutory rape of 44.____
Amy Fisher, has its PRIMARY effect in

   A. punishing the defendant
   B. deterring such acts
   C. showing the public that justice has been meted out
   D. allowing a defendant to plead guilty and walk

45. During a period of probation in which records were kept for 360 children fourteen to eighteen years of age, probation officers found that the group committed certain offenses, as shown in the following table: 45.____

I.Q.	No. of Offenders	No. of Offenses	Offenses Per Offender
61-80	125	338	2.7
81-100	160	448	2.8
101 and over	75	217	2.9

   According to the above data,
   A. the more intelligent offenders are no more law-abiding than, and perhaps not so law-abiding as, the dull offenders
   B. brighter offenders present no more difficult problems than less intelligent offenders
   C. the majority of this probation group is found to be above the average in intelligence of a normal group of young persons within this age range
   D. the relationship between the effectiveness of probation work and the number of offenders is in inverse ratio

46. The fundamental desires for food, shelter, family, and approval, and their accompanying 46.____
instinctive forms of behavior, are among the most important forces in human life because they are essential to and directly connected with the preservation and the welfare of the individual as well as of the race.
According to this statement,

   A. as long as human beings are permitted to act instinctively, they will act wisely
   B. the instinct for self-preservation makes the individual consider his own welfare rather than that of others
   C. racial and individual welfare depend upon the fundamental desires
   D. the preservation of the race demands that instinctive behavior be modified

47. The growth of our cities, the increasing tendency to move from one part of the country to 47.____
another, the existence of people of different cultures in the neighborhood, have together made it more and more difficult to secure group recreation as part of informal family and neighborhood life.
According to this statement,

A. the breaking up of family and neighborhood ties discourages new family and neighborhood group recreation
B. neighborhood recreation no longer forms a significant part of the larger community
C. the growth of cities crowds out the development of all recreational activities
D. the non-English speaking people do not accept new activities easily

48. Sublimation consists in directing some inner urge, arising from a lower psychological level, into some channel of interest on a higher psychological level. Pugnaciousness, for example, is directed into some athletic activity involving combat, such as football or boxing, where rules of fair play and the ethics of the game lift the destructive urge for combat into a constructive experience and offer opportunities for the development of character and personality.
According to this statement,

    A. the manner of self-expression may be directed into constructive activities
    B. athletic activities such as football and boxing are destructive of character
    C. all conscious behavior of high psychological levels indicates the process of sublimation
    D. the rules of fair play are inconsistent with pugnaciousness

49. The interest and curiosity that a child shows in sex matters and activities should be regarded by the probation officer as

    A. a normal interest to be dealt with as one deals with interest in other subjects
    B. something to be disregarded on the assumption that the child will forget about the problem
    C. something to be satisfied by some mythical explanation until the child is old enough to be initiated into the mystery involved
    D. something to be suppressed by threat of punishment

50. When a gang is brought before the court for stealing, the probation officer, in making his pre-probation investigation, should

    A. deal unofficially with the younger ones and officially with the older members of the gang
    B. organize a group of businessmen to take an interest in the members of the gang
    C. recommend that the ringleaders be committed to a child welfare institution and that the others be placed on probation
    D. study each member of the gang and deal with him according to his individual situation

KEY (CORRECT ANSWERS)

1. D	11. B	21. B	31. A	41. D
2. C	12. A	22. D	32. A	42. B
3. C	13. C	23. C	33. B	43. C
4. A	14. C	24. B	34. D	44. C
5. D	15. D	25. B	35. C	45. A
6. B	16. A	26. C	36. D	46. C
7. C	17. A	27. B	37. D	47. A
8. D	18. D	28. B	38. B	48. A
9. B	19. B	29. C	39. D	49. A
10. A	20. A	30. A	40. B	50. D

TEST 2

DIRECTIONS: Each question or incomplete statement is followed by several suggested answers or completions. Select the one that BEST answers the question or completes the statement. *PRINT THE LETTER OF THE CORRECT ANSWER IN THE SPACE AT THE RIGHT.*

1. The one of the following statements which can MOST conceivably be characterized as true is:

    A. Generally speaking, the younger a person is, the less easily he can be influenced by suggestion.
    B. If a probation officer has sufficient technical knowledge of his duties, it is not necessary for him to exercise tact in dealing with criminal offenders.
    C. A probation officer should reject entirely hearsay evidence in making a social diagnosis of a case.
    D. One of the characteristics of adolescence is a feeling in the child that he is misunderstood.

1._____

2. The statement that those parental attitudes are good which offer emotional security to the child BEST expresses the notion that

    A. emotionally secure children do not have feelings of aggression
    B. children should not be held accountable for their actions
    C. parental attitudes are inadequate which do not give the child feelings of belonging and freedom for experience
    D. a family in which there is economic dependence cannot be good for the child

2._____

3. When advised of the need for medical treatment over an extended period of time in a locality some distance from home, the parents of a child with a cardiac ailment decide to send him to a home in another town.
The BEST home for the child in this town would be one

    A. in which there are already residing two foster children who require rest and quiet
    B. in which the family is on relief
    C. in which there are two active boys of the same age as this child
    D. with the bathroom and bedroom on the second floor

3._____

4. Rehabilitation of an offender who has presented serious problems can probably be effected BEST by the probation officer who

    A. believes that the behavior is caused by maladjustment and tries to meet the offender's needs accordingly
    B. is kind and just, but punishes the offender for every lapse of good conduct
    C. keeps the offender under constant observation, making him conscious of his behavior deviations
    D. overlooks minor transgressions and rewards the offender for good behavior

4._____

5. Making an adjustment upon release under probation or parole, as the case may be, is believed by court workers to be EASIER for the

    A. probationer because the delayed action awaiting his release from probation serves to keep him aware of the necessity of continuing his normal life patterns
    B. parolee because he is able to idealize the security of the penitentiary in his recent experience

5._____

C. probationer because he has not been removed from his normal surroundings
D. parolee because frequent visits by family members and close friends during his imprisonment served to provide periodic psychologically uplifting experiences

6. In the granting of probation to a war veteran, the question of leniency on that account should   6.____

   A. not enter because greater leniency to the veteran would give him an unfair advantage over the non-veteran facing the bar with equal guilt
   B. enter because the veteran has made a universally acknowledged contribution to the protection of our society and deserves the protection of his own interests in return
   C. not enter because other important considerations involved in the probation process are the protection of society and the furthering of the best interests of the individual
   D. enter because the military experiences of the veteran may have contributed to his being more irresponsible mentally than the non-veteran

7. During a certain five-year period, it is found that only 66.4 arrests for incest occurred yearly in the city.   7.____
   On the basis of this information, the MOST obvious inference for a probation officer to make is that

   A. the research material on which the data are based is definitely incomplete
   B. apprehension for incest can be expected in about 66.4% of the cases in which this crime is committed
   C. very few cases of incest were committed in the city during the stated period
   D. most cases of incest did not become matters of official police information in the city during the stated period

Questions 8-10.

DIRECTIONS: Questions 8 through 10 are to be answered on the basis of the facts given in the following case history.

<u>Tom Jones</u> - Age 13, I.Q. III

Boy is in 6th grade, school work poor, citizenship fair. He does not constitute a serious behavior problem in school but is often truant.
<u>Relatives</u>

Mother, 33 years of age, divorced father of boy and later remarried. Stepfather and boy did not get along. Stepfather is now out of the home and his whereabouts unknown. Mother is employed in a beauty parlor, earning $255 a week. No other income in family. Woman's mother, age 70, keeps house and looks after boy and his younger sister. Grandmother has absolutely no control over boy.

Sister is 9 years of age, a frail child, never strong, and because of this fact has been *spoiled*.

Boy is undersized, thin, nervous, irritable, and emotional. He likes to read and reads well. Likes WILD WEST and adventure stories. Boy seems fond of his mother. Family lives in a very poor neighborhood.

The mother has an older sister, married, and living on a ranch in Canada. The couple are reported to be fairly well-to-do and have no children. Their ranch is located in a rather remote section. Boy's own father is remarried and living in Seattle. He has two children by his last marriage. Mother is weak and easygoing, passionately fond of both of her children, but inclined to scold them one minute and pet them the next.

Reason Before Court

Boy has been involved with a group of older boys in a series of petty thieveries. Was gone from home for two days at one time and when he returned, told a tale of being kidnapped, which was found later to be entirely imaginary.

8. According to the facts given in the preceding case history, the MOST applicable of the following interpretations for the probation officer to make is

    A. economic factors play a minor part in this case
    B. the boy's taste in reading may indicate a tendency toward instability
    C. removal of the family to a better neighborhood may solve this problem
    D. this is a case for the school authorities to handle because of the truancy involved

9. The conclusion among the following LEAST likely to be reached in a probation report on this case is

    A. the boy's love of adventure and excitement probably contributes to his behavior problem
    B. since the mother lacks stability of character, it would be best to take both children from her
    C. the kidnapping tale, later found to be false, would indicate little possibility of a serious mental defect in the boy
    D. the security of the aunt and uncle's home would be a determining factor in any plan to place the boy with them

10. The one of the following findings LEAST likely to be approved by an experienced probation officer is

    A. the boy can be placed and continued on probation beyond his eighteenth birthday
    B. placement in an *ungraded* class in school might greatly benefit this boy
    C. this family should be referred to a welfare agency in order that the family budget may be supplemented
    D. the greater affection bestowed on the little sister and the consequent jealousy of the boy is probably one of the causes of delinquency

11. The one of the following which is the LEAST valid reason for keeping probation case records is to

    A. maintain an accurate record of the activities of the probationers
    B. meet the legal requirement
    C. provide a record which may be used in appealing from a conviction
    D. provide for continuity of service to the probationer

12. A probation officer is a professional person who has specialized knowledge and skills in the area of casework in an authoritative setting.
    When the period of probation is ended, good probation practice suggests that

    A. the probation officer cease to be interested in the probationer since the case is closed
    B. if there has been a good relationship between officer and probationer, contacts may be continued over a period of years
    C. the probation officer should remain the only person with whom the probationer can feel completely comfortable and confident
    D. the probation officer should maintain continued interest in the probationer so that case files can be built up which may be useful with other probationers

12._____

13. The one of the following which, in cases of juvenile delinquency, is NOT an advantage of probation over commitment to an institution is that probation

    A. offers an individualized form of treatment
    B. is less expensive
    C. gives greater protection to the community
    D. leaves the offender in his normal home surroundings

13._____

14. In order to alleviate the heavy overcrowding of detention homes, a practice sometimes used in the case of a child awaiting a hearing is his confinement in his own home during the hours when he is not engaged in specific authorized pursuits such as attending school or working.
    The one of the following which is LEAST likely to be a serious problem in home detention is the

    A. inability of probation officers or caseworkers to exercise adequate supervision over the child
    B. deprivation of the child from the companionship of children of his age
    C. possibility that the child's family cannot be depended upon to observe the conditions of detention
    D. continual feeling of shame and embarrassment the child may have when in the company of his siblings or friends

14._____

15. Of the following, the CHIEF factor which limits the use of the services of private social casework agencies by probation departments is

    A. the belief by probation departments that the private agencies are unable to give constructive services to the probationers
    B. that the law prohibits use of such services in most types of cases
    C. the reluctance of probationers to accept voluntarily the services of these agencies
    D. the prohibitive cost of these services to the courts

15._____

16. Environmental manipulation as an approach to treatment is often required in probation supervision.
Of the following, the BEST illustration of this approach is a case where the probation officer

   A. adopts a positive rather than a negative attitude toward the client's future after his probation is over
   B. suggests physical changes in the probationer's life and makes referrals to various social agencies for assistance
   C. applies his knowledge of casework techniques in every aspect of probation supervision
   D. cautiously makes use of authority in supervision

17. The disparity in the terms of sentences imposed by different judges in criminal courts for identical crimes has been a cause for serious concern.
Of the following, the GREATEST problem involved in the imposition of sentence is that

   A. the judges do not have any basis on which to impose a sentence other than their own judgment
   B. a serious crime may be punishable by a shorter sentence than a minor offense
   C. some judges will enjoy greater popularity than others
   D. the term of sentence a criminal receives is within the limits set for his crime, dependent on varying standards of the judges

18. In penal administration, *indeterminate sentence* means a

   A. sentence the length of which depends upon the behavior and improvement of the convicted person while in prison
   B. long prison sentence at hard labor
   C. sentence with a minimum and a maximum term determined by the judge within statutory limits
   D. sentence based on circumstantial evidence

19. An agency which provides casework help to parent applicants in deciding whether placement of their children is the solution to the family's problem, and in making referrals to community resources if placement is not indicated, is the

   A. Jewish Child Care Association
   B. Little Flower House
   C. Sheltering Arms Children Service
   D. Wiltwyck School

20. An agency providing casework service with psychiatric consultation and psychological testing for girls including unmarried mothers is the

   A. George Junior Republic
   B. Youth Consultation Service
   C. Goddard Neighborhood Center
   D. Girl's Club

21. Jurisdiction over cases involving the protection and treatment of persons under 16 years of age is vested in the _____ Court.

   A. Family   B. Juvenile   C. Supreme   D. County

22. The basic objective of the Judiciary Article of this state is to establish   22.____

    A. unification of all courts in the city, leaving the courts in the rest of the state unchanged in jurisdiction
    B. a unified court system for the entire state with appropriate jurisdictions in each district
    C. a separate court for each category of cases and a separate category of cases for each court
    D. a statewide court for all civil cases and a statewide court for all criminal cases

23. A caseworker in a city agency is planning to refer one of her clients to a private agency in   23.____
    the community.
    The one of the following which is of GREATEST importance in insuring that the transfer will actually take place is that the

    A. agency is located within the client's proper district
    B. client will cooperate in bringing about such a transfer
    C. caseworker will assure the client that transfer does not mean rejection by the former
    D. agency does not require a fee in excess of what the client can afford

24. The one of the following agencies which provides numerous services to children including recreation, vacation, convalescent care, foster care, and psychiatric service is the   24.____

    A. Child Development Center
    B. Child Welfare League of America
    C. Children's Aid Society
    D. U.S. Children's Bureau

25. Of the following institutions for the chronically ill, the one to which a physically handicapped child would be referred is   25.____

    A. Bird S. Coler Memorial Hospital
    B. Beth Abraham Home
    C. Farm Colony
    D. Josephine Baird Home

26. In planning for the vocational rehabilitation of a physically handicapped person, the use   26.____
    of the sheltered workshop can be a very helpful resource.
    Of the following, the client for whom such service would be MOST appropriate is the one who

    A. will need a constructive way to spend his time for an indefinite period
    B. because of advanced age, is unable to compete in the labor market
    C. needs a transitional experience between his medical care and undertaking a regular job
    D. has a handicap which permanently precludes any gainful employment

27. A group counseling service to parents focused on the understanding of child development and parent-child relations is available through   27.____

    A. Childville
    B. The Arthur Lehman Counseling Service
    C. The State Association for Mental Health
    D. The Child Study Association of America

28. A patient is being discharged from an institutional setting following an initial diagnosis and stabilizing treatment for a diabetic condition of which he had not been aware. His doctor recommends a diet and medication regime for the patient to follow at home, but the patient is uncertain about his ability to carry this out on his own.
A community resource that might be MOST helpful in such a situation is a

    A. visiting nurse service
    B. homemaker service
    C. neighborhood health center
    D. dietitian's service

29. Experience pragmatically suggests that dislocation from cultural roots and customs makes for tension, insecurity, and anxiety. This holds for the child as well as the adolescent, for the new immigrant as well as the second-generation citizen.
Of the following, the MOST important implication of the above statement is that

    A. anxiety, distress, and incapacity are always personal and can be understood best only through an understanding of the child's present cultural environment
    B. in order to resolve the conflicts caused by the displacement of a child from a home with one cultural background to one with another, it is essential that the child fully replace his old culture with the new one
    C. no treatment goal can be envisaged for a dislocated child which does not involve a value judgment which is itself culturally determined
    D. anxiety and distress result from a child's reaction to culturally oriented treatment goals

30. Accepting the fact that mentally gifted children represent superior heredity, the United States faces an important eugenic problem CHIEFLY because

    A. unless these mentally gifted children mature and reproduce more rapidly than the less intelligent children, the nation is heading for a lowering of the average intelligence of its people
    B. although the mentally gifted child always excels scholastically, he generally has less physical stamina than the normal child and tends to lower the nation's population physically
    C. the mentally subnormal are increasing more rapidly than the mentally gifted in America, thus affecting the overall level of achievement of the gifted child
    D. unless the mental level of the general population is raised to that of the gifted child, the mentally gifted will eventually usurp the reigns of government and dominate the mentally weaker

31. The form of psychiatric treatment which requires the LEAST amount of participation on the part of the patient is

    A. psychoanalysis
    B. psychotherapy
    C. shock therapy
    D. non-directive therapy

32. Tests administered by psychologists for the PRIMARY purpose of measuring intelligence are known as _____ tests.

    A. projective
    B. validating
    C. psychometric
    D. apperception

33. In recent years there have been some significant changes in the treatment of patients in state psychiatric hospitals.
These changes are PRIMARILY caused by the use of

   A. electric shock therapy
   B. tranquilizing drugs
   C. steroids
   D. the open ward policy

34. The psychological test which makes use of a set of 20 pictures, each depicting a dramatic scene is known as the

   A. GOODENOUGH TEST
   B. THEMATIC APPERCEPTION TEST
   C. MINNESOTA MULTIPHASIC PERSONALITY INVENTORY
   D. HEALY PICTURE COMPLETION TEST

35. One of the MOST effective ways in which experimental psychologists have been able to study the effects on personality of heredity and environment has been through the study of

   A. primitive cultures
   B. identical twins
   C. mental defectives
   D. newborn infants

36. In hospitals with psychiatric divisions, the psychiatric function is PREDOMINANTLY that of

   A. the training of personnel in all psychiatric disciplines
   B. protection of the community against potentially dangerous psychiatric patients
   C. research and study of psychiatric patients so that new knowledge and information can be made generally available
   D. short-term hospitalization designed to determine diagnosis and recommendations for treatment

37. Predictions of human behavior on the basis of past behavior frequently are inaccurate because

   A. basic patterns of human behavior are in a continual state of flux
   B. human behavior is not susceptible to explanation of a scientific nature
   C. the underlying psychological mechanisms of behavior are not completely understood
   D. quantitative techniques for the measurement of stimuli and responses are unavailable

38. Socio-cultural factors are being re-evaluated in casework practice as they influence both the worker and the client in their participation in the casework process.
Of the following factors, the one which is currently being studied MOST widely is the

   A. social class of worker and client and its significance in casework
   B. difference in native intelligence which can be ascribed to racial origin of an individual
   C. cultural values affecting the areas in which an individual functions
   D. necessity in casework treatment of the client's membership in an organized religious group

39. Deviant behavior is a sociological term used to describe behavior which is not in accord with generally accepted standards. This may include juvenile delinquency, adult criminality, mental or physical illness.
Comparison of normal with deviant behavior is USEFUL because it

    A. makes it possible to establish watertight behavioral descriptions
    B. provides evidence of differential social behavior which distinguishes deviant from normal behavior
    C. indicates that deviant behavior is of no concern to caseworkers
    D. provides no evidence that social role is a determinant of behavior

40. Alcoholism may affect an individual client's ability to function as a spouse, parent, worker, and citizen. Your responsibility to a client with a history of alcoholism is to

    A. interpret to the client the causes of alcoholism as a disease syndrome
    B. work with the alcoholic's family to accept him as he is and to stop trying to reform him
    C. encourage the family of the alcoholic to accept treatment
    D. determine the origins of his particular drinking problem, establish a diagnosis, and work out a treatment plan for him

41. There is a trend to regard narcotic addiction as a form of illness for which the current methods of intervention have not been effective.
Research on the combination of social, psychological, and physical causes of addiction would indicate that social workers should

    A. oppose hospitalization of addicts in institutions
    B. encourage the addict to live normally at home
    C. recognize that there is no successful treatment for addiction and act accordingly
    D. use the existing community facilities differentially for each addict

42. A study of social relationships among delinquent and non-delinquent youth has shown that

    A. delinquent youths generally conceal their true feelings and maintain furtive contacts
    B. delinquents are more impulsive and vivacious than law-abiding boys
    C. non-delinquent youths diminish their active social relationships in order to sublimate any anti-social impulses
    D. delinquent and non-delinquent youths exhibit similar characteristics of impulsiveness and vivaciousness

43. The one of the following which is the CHIEF danger of interpreting the delinquent behavior of a child in terms of morality alone when attempting to get at its causes is that

    A. this tends to overlook the likelihood that the causes of the child's actions are more than a negation of morality and involve varied symptoms of disturbance
    B. a child's moral outlook toward life and society is largely colored by that of his parents, thus encouraging parent-child conflicts
    C. too careful a consideration of the moral aspects of the offense and of the child's needs may often negate the demands of justice in a case
    D. standards of morality may be of no concern to the delinquent and he may not realize the seriousness of his offenses

44. In visiting a school attended by children of a *hard-core* family by your agency, it would generally be ADVISABLE to 44.____

    A. keep the school visit a secret from the family so as not to embarrass the children
    B. encourage the parents to obtain all necessary information themselves
    C. inform the family only if you have secured positive information from the school
    D. have the family fully accept the purpose of the visit beforehand

45. In the process of *reaching out* to service multi-problem families, often many initial appointments are made with adolescents before their parents have received much sustained treatment. 45.____
    This practice is

    A. *undesirable;* adolescents are still subject to parental control and, therefore, the parents should be the focus of treatment
    B. *desirable;* juvenile delinquency is the chief cause of difficulty in multi-problem families
    C. *undesirable;* parental distrust of the worker is increased, thus negating the worker's efforts
    D. *desirable;* adolescents are individual clients and should be so treated

46. A 9-year-old boy is living at home with his remarried, widowed mother, his stepfather, and his 3-year-old half-sister. The boy is being neglected and often severely mistreated by his mother and stepfather. The stepfather resents the boy's presence in the home. 46.____
    After failing to correct the situation by discussions with the boy's mother and stepfather, the caseworker should recommend for the boy's welfare

    A. foster home placement in order to prevent his further mistreatment while corrective educational therapy is used on the parents
    B. permanent separation of the boy from his family as the best means of preventing his continued exposure to the unsatisfactory pressures in the household
    C. placement of the boy outside the household and a stern warning to the parents that similar action will be taken on behalf of the younger child should the situation warrant it
    D. temporary placement of the boy with a foster family until such time as the stepfather is no longer in the household

47. A deserted woman and her 13-year-old son have been receiving public assistance. The woman is drunk most of the time, is known to be consorting with men at all hours, and has been unresponsive to casework treatment. The son has been involved in a few minor incidents which have brought him to the attention of the authorities. 47.____
    The BEST action for the caseworker to take at this point in order to keep the son from becoming an outright delinquent is to recommend that

    A. the mother be arrested and jailed for contributing to the delinquency of a minor and the son be sent to a reformatory
    B. no action be taken against the mother because that will lower her status in the eyes of her son and will further weaken family controls
    C. the son be temporarily placed in a foster home and the mother given treatment for alcoholism
    D. the son be committed to a corrective school where his bad habits can be corrected, since the mother is apparently too sick to assume her responsibilities toward her son

48. A caseworker in a city agency is planning to refer one of her clients to a private agency in the community.
    The one of the following which is of GREATEST importance in insuring that the transfer will actually take place is that the

    A. agency is located within the client's proper district
    B. client will cooperate in bringing about such a transfer
    C. caseworker will assure the client that transfer does not mean rejection by the former
    D. agency does not require a fee in excess of what the client can afford

49. In treating juvenile delinquents, it has been found that there are some who make better social adjustment through group treatment than through an individual casework approach.
    In selecting delinquent boys for group treatment, the one of the following which is the MOST important consideration is that

    A. the boys to be treated in one group be friends or from the same community
    B. only boys who consent to group treatment be included in the group
    C. the ages of the boys included in the group vary as much as possible
    D. only boys who have not reacted to an individual casework approach be included in the group

50. Multi-problem families are generally characterized by various functional indicators.
    Of the following, the family which is MOST likely to be a multi-problem family is one which has

    A. unemployed adult family members
    B. parents with diagnosed character disorders
    C. children and parents with a series of difficulties in the community
    D. poor housekeeping standards

KEY (CORRECT ANSWERS)

1. D	11. C	21. A	31. C	41. D
2. C	12. B	22. B	32. C	42. B
3. A	13. C	23. B	33. B	43. A
4. A	14. B	24. C	34. B	44. D
5. C	15. C	25. A	35. B	45. C
6. C	16. B	26. C	36. D	46. A
7. D	17. D	27. D	37. C	47. C
8. C	18. C	28. A	38. C	48. B
9. B	19. A	29. C	39. B	49. B
10. A	20. B	30. A	40. D	50. C

EXAMINATION SECTION
TEST 1

DIRECTIONS: Each question or incomplete statement is followed by several suggested answers or completions. Select the one that BEST answers the question or completes the statement. *PRINT THE LETTER OF THE CORRECT ANSWER IN THE SPACE AT THE RIGHT.*

1. When a counselee describes a problem which is similar to one the counselor has had, the counselor usually should

   A. tell the counselee how he reacted in similar circumstances
   B. suggest solutions which worked for him
   C. describe his own experiences, but disguise them by saying they happened to another of his counselees
   D. make no reference to his experience

2. Of the following, the MOST highly specialized process in guidance is

   A. testing
   B. occupational study
   C. interviewing
   D. counseling

3. Which of the following is the MOST fundamental aim of guidance?

   A. Solve client's problems
   B. Counsel clients concerning problems
   C. Develop self-direction
   D. Direct the client to strive for excellence

4. A counselor forecasts the extent to which the counselee may or may not make a desirable or satisfying adaptation to his situation. Williamson referred to this step in the counseling process as

   A. synthesis
   B. prognosis
   C. follow-up
   D. diagnosis

5. A fundamental assumption made by the client-centered school of counseling is that

   A. diagnosis is essential to effective counseling
   B. every individual possesses a "tendency toward growth"
   C. responsibility for client actions is assumed by the counselor
   D. the counselor's role is primarily one of giving information to the counselee

6. Referral of a client to other agencies should be made

   A. after a long period of counseling has proved ineffectual
   B. only with the client's and his parent's consent
   C. as soon as the needed adjustment lies outside of client's, as well as counselor's, control
   D. after consultation with teachers and administration

7. According to field theory, individuals who are initially faced with a problem tend to seek

   A. long involved indirect solutions
   B. simple direct solutions
   C. outside help in forcing a solution
   D. means of withdrawing from the problem

8. In regard to client activity, the goal of counseling agreed upon by all methodologies is

   A. integrated controlled behavior
   B. release of feeling and negative emotion
   C. more individuals who understand themselves
   D. conformity to the cultural mores

9. A counselor who is primarily concerned with analyzing and diagnosing a client's problems, collecting and synthesizing data about the client, and making predictions about the consequences of various client decisions would BEST be classified as using which method of counseling? The

   A. *clinical* method as described by Williamson
   B. *client-centered* method as described by Rogers
   C. *communications* method as described by Robinson
   D. *learning* method as described by Dollard & Miller

10. Most definitions would NOT include which of the following as a necessary aspect of counseling?

    A. The counselor and client meet face-to-face.
    B. The client is experiencing a degree of emotional disturbance.
    C. A unique learning opportunity is provided for the client.
    D. The counselor brings special competence to the counseling relationship.

11. The *initial* counseling interview is considered by many to be hardest.
    Which one of the following is NOT an essential objective of this session? To

    A. develop a sound working relationship with the individual
    B. make a diagnosis of the client's problem
    C. orient the client to the nature of the counseling process
    D. provide an atmosphere that allows the individual to express freely his attitudes and feelings

12. A powerful dynamic in the counseling process and usually the very antithesis of its counterpart in the instructional process is

    A. encouraging accuracy
    B. emphasizing structure
    C. encouraging sequential orderly thinking
    D. processing ambiguity

13. Counseling techniques are useful in working with advantaged, bright or creative children. Fundamental is a counseling atmosphere that is

    A. non-threatening
    B. urging for creativity
    C. highly charged to stimulate excitement
    D. pretty well structured

14. Which one of the following counseling approaches emphasizes differential diagnosis in the treatment of individual clients?

    A. Trait- and factor-centered
    B. Self-theory
    C. Communications
    D. Psychoanalytic

15. The school of counseling theory, characterized by the attempt to observe behavior from the point of view of the individual himself (i.e., his own frame of reference), is known as

    A. organismic
    B. neo-Freudianism
    C. existentialism
    D. phenomenology

16. Of the following, which characteristic do counseling theorists consider MOST essential to the effectiveness of a counselor?

    A. Extroversion
    B. Persuasiveness
    C. Serenity
    D. Objectivity

17. The counseling approach which uses any of a variety of techniques which BEST suit individual situations is called

    A. instinctive
    B. specific
    C. conditioning
    D. eclectic

18. Mental testing, statistics, and measurement are identified *most closely* with which one of the following counseling approaches?

    A. Neobehavioral
    B. Trait- and factor-centered
    C. Psychoanalytic
    D. Communications

19. The "self-actualization" process is the central tendency of which one of the following approaches in counseling?

    A. Neobehavioral
    B. Communications
    C. Self-theory
    D. Psychoanalytic

20. In counseling, the LEAST acceptable introduction in phrasing an interpretative statement is which one of the following?

    A. "It seems as though..."
    B. "Do you suppose that..."
    C. "It probably would be better if..."
    D. "I'm wondering if..."

21. The term "ambiguity" in counseling refers to the degree of, openness or uncertainty that exists in the minds of both counselor and client regarding what is supposed to happen next.
    The ULTIMATE degree of ambiguity in counseling is represented by the use of

    A. open-ended leads
    B. depth interpretation
    C. "yes" and "no" questions
    D. free association

22. The client says, "I can't seem to get along with the other kids."
    Of the following, the MOST appropriate counselor response is:

    A. "Have you done your part?"
    B. "Let's talk about it."
    C. "You're too reserved and too cold."
    D. "You don't care very much about it."

23. In psychoanalytically-oriented counseling, the responsibility for the client's bringing up and talking about important material lies

    A. *exclusively* with the client
    B. *primarily* with the client, with the help of the counselor
    C. *primarily* with the counselor, with the cooperation of the client
    D. *exclusively* with the counselor

24. Research shows that, regardless of theoretical persuasion, experienced counselors as compared with less experienced counselors tend to

    A. use a wider range of techniques
    B. rely primarily on reflection of feeling
    C. use deeper interpretations
    D. take more responsibility for content

25. STRUCTURING in counseling is the process of

    A. building rapport in the initial interview
    B. establishing the ground rules for the counselor
    C. determining the client's real problem
    D. communicating and sharing expectations about counseling

KEY (CORRECT ANSWERS)

1.	D	11.	B
2.	D	12.	D
3.	C	13.	A
4.	B	14.	A
5.	B	15.	D
6.	C	16.	D
7.	B	17.	D
8.	A	18.	B
9.	A	19.	C
10.	B	20.	C

21. D
22. B
23. B
24. A
25. D

TEST 2

DIRECTIONS: Each question or incomplete statement is followed by several suggested answers or completions. Select the one that BEST answers the question or completes the statement. *PRINT THE LETTER OF THE CORRECT ANSWER IN THE SPACE AT THE RIGHT.*

1. Of non-white youngsters in the United States who drop out before completing 4 years of high school, what proportion come from families earning less than $20,000?

    A. 25% B. 40% C. Over 50% D. Over 90%

2. Educational attainment has been rising. Median school years of attainment for persons now holding clerical or sales jobs average

    A. more than 12 years B. less than 12 years
    C. more than 10 years D. less than 10 years

3. From the client-centered point of view of counseling, information about the client's skills, personality, etc. are best used

    A. to help the counselor to understand the client better
    B. to help the client to understand himself better
    C. as a basis for the counselor's suggestions, which the client is free to reject
    D. as a part of the counselor's diagnosis in deciding how best to work with the client

4. Appropriate responses for a counselor include all of the following EXCEPT

    A. "If I were you..."
    B. "Can you tell me more about...?"
    C. "How do you feel about...?"
    D. "How long has this been going on...?"

5. During the early stages of a counseling relationship, a client engages in long periods of silence and appears to have difficulty in discussing questions which the counselor raises. A psychoanalytically-oriented counselor would *probably* interpret these silences and difficulties as signs of

    A. lack of rapport
    B. frustrated oral needs
    C. the client's inability to analyze his problems
    D. resistance to dealing with emotional problems

6. The single recent book which focuses specifically on problems of professionalization in counseling in the present society and makes dramatic recommendations for counselor training is THE COUNSELOR IN A CHANGING WORLD. The author is

    A. Dugald S. Arbuckle B. Edward C. Glanz
    C. Leslie E. Moser   D. C. Gilbert Wrenn

7. All of above the following are identified with existential counseling EXCEPT

    A. Frankl   B. May
    C. Van Kamm   D. Eysenck

8. In the final analysis, realization of potential by the individual depends upon

   A. his abilities
   B. the limits imposed by his society and culture
   C. subjective interactional factors
   D. all of the above

9. Which one of the following is the MOST important deterrent to evaluation of guidance programs? Lack of

   A. objective data
   B. suitable criteria
   C. research skills among guidance workers
   D. data processing equipment

10. Acculturation, the process of acquiring values different from those of the culture into which one is born, can BEST be promoted through guidance of

    A. introducing the student to the new culture
    B. showing the student how the culture into which he was born is inadequate
    C. supporting the individual in learning the new culture and by rewarding him for the new learning
    D. showing the student that cultural differences are relatively unimportant

11. The client speaks so low that you cannot hear what he is saying.
    The BEST technique to use in handling this would be to

    A. confront the client with the problem
    B. pretend that you can hear him
    C. respond in like manner
    D. interpret this action to him as an "interpersonal defense mechanism"

12. All of the following are important in the "social-psychological" theories of counseling EXCEPT

    A. life style
    B. cognitive processes
    C. interpersonal relationships
    D. need for identity

13. In distinguishing between counseling and clinical psychology, which of the following tends to be TRUE of the counselor but not of the clinician?

    A. The major focus is on the normal, adaptive resources of the client's personality
    B. The use of psychological test data to contribute to a better understanding of the client
    C. A supportive and accepting relationship is developed
    D. The disintegrative, disturbed aspects of the client's personality receive major attention

14. Which of the following words is MOST similar in meaning to "reliability"?

    A. Consistency   B. Interpretability
    C. Objectivity   D. Truthfulness

15. Which of the following can be classified as an observational device?

    A. Anecdotal records
    B. Interest inventories
    C. Projective technique
    D. Personality inventories

16. As a guidance counselor, you may often be consulted by parents about how to respond more helpfully to teenagers. Which one of the following judgments about parent-teenager relationships is false?

    A. Parents' approval of work well done and pride in accomplishment means a great deal to the teenager, even though he brushes it off.
    B. For the sake of the young person's self-respect, it is a good idea to criticize him as much as possible.
    C. Giving a teenager opportunity for being in with a group is closely related to school progress.
    D. Parents' recognition and appreciation of good school progress, without putting on heavy pressure, is a help in keeping it up

17. In counseling, the term "understanding" refers to

    A. the counselor's ability to communicate how a client's behavior appears to other people
    B. the counselor's skill in grasping meanings the client's comments convey
    C. the counselor's adeptness in anticipating feelings of the client
    D. the counselor's knowledge of dynamics of personality

18. Of the following, the MOST significant difference between "psychotherapy" and "counseling" is in the

    A. goals and expected outcomes
    B. techniques used
    C. amount of psychological insight involved
    D. professional background of the counselor

19. Appropriate "bridges" for the counselor in counseling are all of the following EXCEPT

    A. "Let's move on to..."
    B. "We were talking about..."
    C. "What was it you said about...?"
    D. "How does this fit in with what you said earlier?"

20. From the client-centered point of view, "understanding" in counseling is BEST thought of as

    A. diagnosing the client's motivational structure
    B. seeing the client's world as he sees it
    C. following and accepting the client's spoken words
    D. the ability to predict future actions

21. The statement of a client MOST indicative of *transference* feelings is:

    A. "I really didn't feel like coming here today."
    B. "My mother doesn't approve of my talking to you."
    C. "If only you would tell me what I should do."
    D. "You remind me of my father."

22. In counseling, "reflection" refers to 22.____

    A. a restatement of the counselee's comment
    B. clarification of the content of the remark
    C. the counselor's perception of the feelings being expressed
    D. a non-committal statement such as "uh huh"

23. In the given paradigm, all are CORRECTLY matched EXCEPT: 23.____

	Counseling Model	Predominant Goal
A.	Psychoanalytic	insight
B.	Teacher-learner	sound decision and self-understanding
C.	Behavioral	shaping of specific responses
D.	Client-centered	catharsis

24. Freud believes that the client builds defenses against his inner conflicts when the therapeutic process tempts him to express conflictual impulses. These defenses result in resistance. 24.____
    According to Freud, such resistance in successful counseling

    A. is unavoidable
    B. is carefully avoided by the counselor
    C. indicates the counselor has proceeded too fast
    D. does not occur

25. Existential counseling includes all of the following characteristics EXCEPT 25.____

    A. a belief in universal values
    B. a subjective view of reality
    C. the total empathic response of the therapist
    D. the individual's intense awareness of his contingency and his freedom

KEY (CORRECT ANSWERS)

1. C
2. A
3. B
4. A
5. D

6. D
7. D
8. D
9. B
10. C

11. A
12. B
13. A
14. A
15. A

16. B
17. B
18. A
19. A
20. B

21. D
22. C
23. D
24. A
25. A

INTERVIEWING EXAMINATION SECTION
TEST 1

DIRECTIONS: Each question or incomplete statement is followed by several suggested answers or completions. Select the one that BEST answers the question or completes the statement. *PRINT THE LETTER OF THE CORRECT ANSWER IN THE SPACE AT THE RIGHT.*

1. You are conducting an interview with a client who has been having some difficulties with one of her fellow-workers. The client walks on crutches. You tell the client that she probably finds it difficult to get along with her fellow-workers because of this handicap.
   To make such a statement would, *generally*, be

   A. *proper;* people are often prejudiced against persons with physical deformities
   B. *proper;* statements such as this indicate to the client that you are sympathetic toward her
   C. *improper;* this approach would not help the client solve her problem
   D. *improper;* you should have discussed this handicap in relation to the client's continued ability to continue in her job

   1.____

2. The information which the interviewer plans to secure from an individual with whom he talks is determined MAINLY by the

   A. purpose of the interview and the functions of the agency
   B. state assistance laws and the desires of the individual
   C. privacy they have while talking and the willingness of the individual to give information
   D. emotional feelings of the individual seeking help and the interviewer's reactions to these feelings

   2.____

3. *Generally,* the MOST effective of the following ways of dealing with a person being interviewed who frequently digresses from the subject under discussion or starts to ramble, is for the interviewer to

   A. tell the person that he, the interviewer, will have to terminate the interview unless the former sticks to the point
   B. increase the tempo of the interview
   C. demonstrate that he is a good listener and allow the person to continue in his own way
   D. inject questions which relate to the purpose of the interview

   3.____

4. "Being a good listener" is an interviewing technique which, if applied properly, is *desirable* MOSTLY because it

   A. catches the client more easily in misrepresentations and lies
   B. conserves the energies of the interviewer
   C. encourages the client to talk about his personal affairs without restraint
   D. encourages the giving of information which is generally more reliable and complete

   4.____

5. When questioning applicants for eligibility, it would be BEST to ask questions that are

   5.____

A. *direct,* so that the applicant will realize that the interviewer knows what he is doing
B. *direct,* so that the information received will be as pertinent as possible
C. *indirect,* so that the applicant will not realize the purpose of the interview
D. *indirect,* so that you can trap the applicant into making admissions that he would not otherwise make

6. The CHIEF reason for conducting an interview with a new applicant in complete privacy is that the

   A. interviewer will be better able to record the facts without any other worker reading his case notes
   B. applicant will be impressed by the business-like atmosphere of the agency
   C. interviewer will be able to devote more time to questioning the applicant without interruption
   D. applicant will be more likely to speak frankly

7. When conducting an interview with a client who is upset because of an increase in rent, it would be BEST for the interviewer to

   A. agree with the client that the agency was wrong in raising his rent, as a basis for further discussion
   B. tell the client that unless he calms down the interview will be ended
   C. prevent the client from becoming emotional
   D. tell the client the reasons for the increase

8. At an interview to determine whether an applicant is eligible, the applicant gives information different from that which he submitted on his application.
The MOST advisable action to take is to

   A. cross out the old information, enter the new information, and initial the entry
   B. re-enter the old information on the application form and initial the entry
   C. give the applicant another application form, have him fill it out correctly, and resume the interview
   D. give the applicant another application form to fill out, and set a later date for another interview

9. After you have secured, in an interview, all the necessary information from an applicant, he shows no intention of leaving, but starts to tell you a long personal story.
Of the following, the MOST advisable action for you to take is to

   A. explain to the applicant why personal stories are out of place in a business office
   B. listen carefully to the story for whatever relevant information it may contain
   C. interrupt him tactfully, thank him for the information he has already given, and terminate the interview
   D. inform your supervisor that the time required for this interview will prevent you from completing the interviews scheduled for the day

10. In interviewing, the practice of anticipating an applicant's answers to questions is, *generally,*

    A. *desirable* because it is effective and economical when it is necessary to interview large numbers of applicants
    B. *desirable* because many applicants have language difficulties

C. *undesirable* because it is the inalienable right of every person to answer as he sees fit
D. *undesirable* because applicants may tend to agree with the answer proposed by the interviewer even when the answer is not entirely correct

11. A follow-up interview was arranged for an applicant in order that he might furnish certain requested evidence. At this follow-up interview, the applicant still fails to furnish the necessary evidence.
It would be MOST advisable for you to

   A. advise the applicant that he is now considered ineligible
   B. ask the applicant how soon he can get the necessary evidence and set a date for another interview
   C. question the applicant carefully and thoroughly to determine if he has misrepresented or falsified any information
   D. set a date for another interview and tell the applicant to get the necessary evidence by that time

12. When an initial interview is being conducted, one way of starting is to explain the purpose of the interview to the applicant.
The practice of starting the interview with such an explanation is, *generally,*

   A. *desirable* because the applicant can then understand why the interview is necessary and what will be accomplished by it
   B. *desirable* because it creates the rapport which is necessary to successful interviewing
   C. *undesirable* because time will be saved by starting off directly with the questions which must be asked
   D. *undesirable* because the interviewer should have the choice of starting an interview in any manner he prefers

13. Empathy can be defined as the ability of one individual to respond sensitively and imaginatively to another's feelings.
For an interviewer to be empathic during an interview is *usually*

   A. *undesirable,* mainly because an interviewer should never be influenced by the feelings of the one being interviewed
   B. *desirable,* mainly because an interview will not be productive unless the interviewer takes the side of the person interviewed
   C. *undesirable,* mainly because empathy usually leads an interviewer to be biased in favor of the person being interviewed
   D. *desirable,* mainly because this ability allows the interviewer to direct his questions more effectively to the person interviewed

14. Assume that you must interview several people who know each other.
To gather them all in one group and question them TOGETHER, is, *generally,*

   A. *good practice,* since any inaccurate information offered by one person would be corrected by others in the group
   B. *poor practice,* since people in a group rarely pay adequate attention to questions
   C. *good practice,* since the interviewer will save much time and effort in this way
   D. *poor practice,* since the presence of several people can inhibit an individual from speaking

15. An effective interviewer should know that the one of the following reasons which LEAST describes why there is a wide range of individual behavior in human relations is that

    A. socio-economic status influences human behavior
    B. physical characteristics do not influence human behavior
    C. education influences human behavior
    D. childhood experience influences human behavior

16. An interviewer encounters an uncooperative interviewee. Of the following, the FIRST thing the interviewer should do in such a situation is to

    A. try various appeals to win the interviewee over to a cooperative attitude
    B. try to ascertain the reason for non-cooperation
    C. promise the interviewee that all data will be kept confidential
    D. alter his interviewing technique with the uncooperative interviewee

17. You discover that an interviewee who was requested to bring with him specific documents for his initial employment interview has forgotten the documents.
    Of the following, the BEST course of action to take is to

    A. give the person a reasonable amount of time to furnish the documents
    B. tell the person you will let him know how much additional time he has
    C. mark the person disqualified for employment; he has failed to provide reasonably requested data on time
    D. mark the person provisionally qualified for employment; upon receipt of the documents he will be permanently qualified

18. In checking interviewees' work experience, you realize that the person whom you are to interview is only marginally fluent in English and has, therefore, requested permission to bring a translator with him.
    Of the following, the BEST course of action is to inform the interviewee that

    A. outside translators may not be used
    B. only city translators may be used
    C. state law requires fluency in English of all civil servants
    D. he may be assisted in the interview by his translator

19. Assume that, during the course of an interview, you are verbally attacked by the person being interviewed.
    Of the following, it would be MOST advisable to

    A. answer back in a matter-of-fact manner
    B. ask the person to apologize and discontinue the interview
    C. ignore the attack but adjourn the interview to another day
    D. use restraint and continue the interview

20. Assume that you find that the person you are interviewing has difficulty finishing his sentences and seems to be groping for words.
    In such a case, the BEST approach for you to take is to

    A. say what you think the person has in mind
    B. proceed patiently without calling attention to the problem
    C. ask the person why he finds it difficult to finish his sentences
    D. interrupt the interview until the person feels more relaxed

21. The one of the following which BEST describes the effect of the *sympathetic approach* in interviewing on the interviewee is that it will

    A. have no discernible effect on the interviewee
    B. calm the interviewee
    C. lead the interviewee to underemphasize his problems
    D. mislead the interviewee

22. The one of the following characteristics which is a PRIMARY requisite for a successful interview is

    A. total *curiosity*
    B. total *sympathy*
    C. complete *attention*
    D. complete *dedication*

23. Assume that you have been assigned to conduct a follow-up interview with a primary witness.
    The one of the following which is MOST important in arranging such an interview is to

    A. keep the witness cooperative
    B. conduct the matter in secret
    C. allow the witness to determine where and when the interview takes place
    D. conduct the interview as soon as possible to insure a strong case

24. By examining a candidate's employment record, an interviewer can determine many things about the candidate. Of the following, the one which is LEAST apparent from an employment record is the candidate's

    A. character
    B. willingness to work
    C. capacity to get along with co-workers
    D. potential for advancing in civil service

25. Assume that you are conducting an interview in which the person being interviewed is using the interview as a forum for venting his anti-civil service feelings.
    Of the following, the FIRST thing that you should do is to

    A. agree with the person; perhaps that will shorten the outburst
    B. respectfully disagree with the person; the decorum of the interview has already been disrupted
    C. courteously and objectively direct the interview to the relevant issue
    D. reschedule the interview to another mutually agreeable time

KEY (CORRECT ANSWERS)

1. C
2. A
3. D
4. D
5. B

6. D
7. D
8. A
9. C
10. D

11. B
12. A
13. D
14. D
15. B

16. B
17. A
18. D
19. D
20. B

21. C
22. C
23. A
24. D
25. C

TEST 2

DIRECTIONS: Each question or incomplete statement is followed by several suggested answers or completions. Select the one that BEST answers the question or completes the statement. *PRINT THE LETTER OF THE CORRECT ANSWER IN THE SPACE AT THE RIGHT.*

1. The pattern of an interview is LARGELY set by the

    A. person being interviewed
    B. person conducting the interview
    C. nature of the interview
    D. policy of the agency employing the interviewer

2. Assume that a person being interviewed, who had been talking freely, suddenly tries to change the subject.
   To a trained interviewer, this behavior would mean that the person *probably*

    A. knew very little about the subject
    B. realized that he was telling too much
    C. decided that his privacy was being violated
    D. realized that he was becoming confused

3. Assume that you receive a telephone call from an unknown individual requesting information about a person you are currently interviewing.
   In such a situation, the BEST course of action for you to take is to

    A. give him the information over the telephone
    B. tell him to write to your department for the information
    C. send him the information, retaining a copy for your files
    D. tell him to call back, giving you additional time to check into the matter

4. In an interview, assuming that the interviewer was using a *non-directive approach* in this interview, of the following, the interviewer's most effective response would be:

    A. "You know, you are building a bad record of tardiness."
    B. "Can you tell me more about this situation?"
    C. "What kind of person is your superior?"
    D. "Do you think you are acting fairly towards the agency by being late so often?"

5. In an interview, assuming that the interviewer was using a *directed approach* in this interview, of the following, the interviewer's response should be:

    A. "That doesn't seem like much of an excuse to me."
    B. "What do you mean by saying that you've lost interest?"
    C. "What problems are there with the supervision you are getting?"
    D. "How do you think your tardiness looks in your personnel record?"

Questions 6-8.

DIRECTIONS: Answer Questions 6 through 8 only on the basis of information given in the passage below.

A personnel interviewer, selecting job applicants, may find that he reacts badly to some people even on first contact. This reaction cannot usually be explained by things that the interviewee has done or said. Most of us have had the experience of liking or disliking, of feeling comfortable or uncomfortable with people on first acquaintance, long before we have had a chance to make a conscious, rational decision about them. Often, too, our liking or disliking is transmitted to the other person by subtle processes such as gestures, posture, voice intonations, or choice of words. The point to be kept in mind in this: the relations between people are complex and occur at several levels, from the conscious to the unconscious. This is true whether the relationship is brief or long, formal or informal.

Some of the major dynamics of personality which operate on the unconscious level are projection, sublimation, rationalization, and repression. Encountering these for the first time, one is apt to think of them as representing pathological states. In the extreme, they undoubtedly are, but they exist so universally that we must consider them also to be parts of normal personality.

Without necessarily subscribing to any of the numerous theories of personality, it is possible to describe personality in terms of certain important aspects or elements. We are all aware of ourselves as thinking organisms.

This aspect of personality, the conscious part, is important for understanding human behavior, but it is not enough. Many find it hard to accept the notion that each person also has an unconscious. The existence of the unconscious is no longer a matter of debate. It is not possible to estimate at all precisely what proportion of our total psychological life is conscious, what proportion unconscious. Everyone who has studied the problem, however, agrees that consciousness is the smaller part of personality. Most of what we are and do is a result of unconscious processes. To ignore this is to risk mistakes.

6. The passage above suggests that an interviewer can be MOST effective if he

   A. learns how to determine other peoples' unconscious motivations
   B. learns how to repress his own unconsciously motivated mannerisms and behavior
   C. can keep others from feeling that he either likes or dislikes them
   D. gains an understanding of how the unconscious operates in himself and in others

7. It may be inferred from the passage above that the "subtle processes, such as gestures, posture, voice intonation, or choice of words," referred to in the first paragraph, are, *usually*,

   A. in the complete control of an expert interviewer
   B. the determining factors in the friendships a person establishes
   C. controlled by a person's unconscious
   D. not capable of being consciously controlled

8. The passage above implies that various different personality theories are, *usually*,

   A. so numerous and different as to be valueless to an interviewer
   B. in basic agreement about the importance of the unconscious
   C. understood by the interviewer who strives to be effective
   D. in agreement that personality factors such as projection and repression are pathological

Questions 9-10.

DIRECTIONS: Answer Questions 9 and 10 ONLY on the basis of information given in the passage below.

    Since we generally assure informants that what they say is confidential, we are not free to tell one informant what the other has told us. Even if the informant says, "I don't care who knows it; tell anybody you want to," we find it wise to treat the interview as confidential. An interviewer who relates to some informants what other informants have told him is likely to stir up anxiety and suspicion. Of course, the interviewer may be able to tell an informant what he has heard without revealing the source of his information. This may be perfectly appropriate where a story has wide currency so that an informant cannot infer the source of the information. But if an event is not widely known, the mere mention of it may reveal to one informant what another informant has said about the situation. How can the data be cross-checked in these circumstances?

9. The passage above implies that the anxiety and suspicion an interviewer may arouse by telling what has been learned in other interviews is due to the

    A. lack of trust the person interviewed may have in the interviewer's honesty
    B. troublesome nature of the material which the interviewer has learned in other interviews
    C. fact that the person interviewed may not believe that permission was given to repeat the information
    D. fear of the person interviewed that what he is telling the interviewer will be repeated

10. The paragraph above is *most likely* part of a longer passage dealing with

    A. ways to verify data gathered in interviews
    B. the various anxieties a person being interviewed may feel
    C. the notion that people sometimes say things they do not mean
    D. ways an interviewer can avoid seeming suspicious

Questions 11-12.

DIRECTIONS: Answer Questions 11 and 12 ONLY on the basis of information given below.

    The ability to interview rests not only on any single trait, but on a vast complex of them. Habits, skills, techniques, and attitudes are all involved. Competence in interviewing is acquired only after careful and diligent study, prolonged practice (preferably under supervision), and a good bit of trial and error; for interviewing is not an exact science, it is an art. Like many other arts, however, it can and must draw on science in several of its aspects.

    There is always a place for individual initiative, for imaginative innovations, and for new combinations of old approaches. The skilled interviewer cannot be bound by a set of rules. Likewise, there is not a set of rules which can guarantee to the novice that his interviewing will be successful. There are, however, some accepted, general guide-posts which may help the beginner to avoid mistakes, learn how to conserve his efforts, and establish effective working relationships with interviewees; to accomplish, in short, what he set out to do.

11. According to the passage above, rules and standard techniques for interviewing are

A. helpful for the beginner, but useless for the experienced, innovative interviewer
B. destructive of the innovation and initiative needed for a good interviewer
C. useful for even the experienced interviewer, who may, however, sometimes go beyond them
D. the means by which nearly anybody can become an effective interviewer

12. According to the passage above, the one of the following which is a prerequisite to competent interviewing is   12.____

    A. avoiding mistakes   B. study and practice
    C. imaginative innovation   D. natural aptitude

Questions 13-16.

DIRECTIONS: Answer Questions 13 through 16 SOLELY on the basis of information given in the following paragraph.

   The question of what material is relevant is not as simple as it might seem. Frequently material which seems irrelevant to the inexperienced has, because of the common tendency to disguise and distort and misplace one's feelings, considerable significance. It may be necessary to let the client "ramble on" for a while in order to clear the decks, as it were, so that he may get down to things that really are on his mind. On the other hand, with an already disturbed person, it may be important for the interviewer to know when to discourage further elaboration of upsetting material. This is especially the case where the worker would be unable to do anything about it. An inexperienced interviewer might, for instance, be intrigued with the bizarre elaboration of material that the psychotic produces, but further elaboration of this might encourage the client in his instability. A too random discussion may indicate that the interviewee is not certain in what areas the interviewer is prepared to help him, and he may be seeking some direction. Or again, satisfying though it may be for the interviewer to have the interviewee tell him intimate details, such revelations sometimes need to be checked or encouraged only in small doses. An interviewee who has "talked too much" often reveals subsequent anxiety. This is illustrated by the fact that? frequently after a "confessional" interview ,the interviewee surprises the interviewer by being withdrawn, inarticulate, or hostile, or by breaking the next appointment.

13. Sometimes a client may reveal certain personal information to an interviewer and subsequently, may feel anxious about this revelation.   13.____
    If, during an interview, a client begins to discuss very personal matters, it would be BEST to

    A. tell the client, in no uncertain terms, that you're not interested in personal details
    B. ignore the client at this point
    C. encourage the client to elaborate further on the details
    D. inform the client that the information seems to be very personal

14. Clients with severe psychological disturbances pose an especially difficult problem for the inexperienced interviewer.
    The difficulty lies in the possibility of the client's

    A. becoming physically violent and harming the interviewer
    B. "rambling on" for a while
    C. revealing irrelevant details which may be followed by cancelled appointments
    D. reverting to an unstable state as a result of interview material

14._____

15. An interviewer should be constantly alert to the possibility of obtaining clues from the client as to problem areas.
    According to the above passage, a client who discusses topics at random may be

    A. unsure of what problems the interviewer can provide help
    B. reluctant to discuss intimate details
    C. trying to impress the interviewer with his knowledge
    D. deciding what relevant material to elaborate on

15._____

16. The evaluation of a client's responses may reveal substantial information that may aid the interviewer in assessing the problem areas that are of concern to the client. Responses that seemed irrelevant at the time of the interview may be of significance because

    A. considerable significance is attached to all irrelevant material
    B. emotional feelings are frequently masked
    C. an initial "rambling on" is often a prelude to what -is actually bothering the client
    D. disturbed clients often reveal subsequent anxiety

16._____

Questions 17-19.

DIRECTIONS: Answer Questions 17 through 19 SOLELY on the basis of the following paragraph.

The physical setting of the interview may determine its entire potentiality. Some degree of privacy and a comfortable relaxed atmosphere are important. The interviewee is not encouraged to give much more than his name and address if the interviewer seems busy with other things, if people are rushing about, if there are distracting noises. He has a right to feel that, whether the interview lasts five minutes or an hour, he has, for that time, the undivided attention of the interviewer. Interruptions, telephone calls, and so on, should be reduced to a minimum. If the interviewee has waited in a crowded room for what seems to him an interminably long period, he is naturally in no mood to sit down and discuss what is on his mind. Indeed, by that time the primary thing on his mind may be his irritation at being kept waiting, and he frequently feels it would be impolite to express this. If a wait or interruptions have been unavoidable, it is always helpful to give the client some recognition that these are disturbing and that he can naturally understand that they make it more difficult for him to proceed. At the same time if he protests that they have not troubled him, the interviewer can best accept his statements at their face value, as further insistence that they must have been disturbing may be interpreted by him as accusing, and he may conclude that the interviewer has been personally hurt by his irritation.

17. Distraction during an interview may tend to limit the client's responses. 17.____
In a case where an interruption has occurred, it would be BEST for the interviewer to

   A. terminate this interview and have it rescheduled for another time period
   B. ignore the interruption since it is not continuous
   C. express his understanding that the distraction can cause the client to feel disturbed
   D. accept the client's protests that he has been troubled by the interruption

18. To maximize the rapport that can be established with the client, an appropriate physical 18.____
setting is necessary. At the very least, some privacy would be necessary.
In addition, the interviewer should

   A. always appear to be busy in order to impress the client
   B. focus his attention only on the client
   C. accept all the client's statements as being valid
   D. stress the importance of the interview to the client

19. Clients who have been waiting quite some time for their interview may, justifiably, become 19.____
upset. However, a client *may initially* attempt to mask these feelings because he may

   A. personally hurt the interviewer
   B. want to be civil
   C. feel that the wait was unavoidable
   D. fear the consequences of his statement

20. You have been assigned to interview W, a witness, concerning a minor automobile acci- 20.____
dent. Although you have made no breach of the basic rules of contact and approach,
you, nevertheless, recognize that you and W have a personality clash and that a natural
animosity has resulted.
Of the following, you MOST appropriately should

   A. discuss the personality problem with W and attempt to resolve the difference
   B. stop the interview on some pretext and leave in a calm and pleasant manner, allowing an associate to continue the interview
   C. ignore the personality problem and continue as though nothing had happened
   D. change the subject matter being discussed since the facts sought may be the source of the animosity

21. Assume that you desire to interview W, a reluctant witness to an event that took place 21.____
several weeks previously. Assume further that the interview can take place at a location
to be designated by the interviewer.
Of the following, the place of interview should *preferably* be the

   A. office of the interviewer
   B. home of W
   C. office of W
   D. scene where the event took place

22. Assume that you are interviewing W, a witness. During the interview it becomes apparent 22.____
that W's statements are inaccurate and at variance with the facts previously established.
In these circumstances, it would be BEST for you to

   A. tell W that his statements are inaccurate and point out how they conflict with previously established facts

B. reword your questions and ask additional questions about the facts being discussed
C. warn W that he may be required to testify under oath at a later date
D. ignore W's statements if you have other information that support the facts

23. Assume that W, a witness being interviewed by you, shows a tendency to ramble. His answers to your questions are lengthy and not responsive.
In this situation, the BEST action for you to take is to

    A. permit W to continue because at some point he will tell you the information sought
    B. tell W that he is rambling and unresponsive and that more will be accomplished if he is brief and to the point
    C. control the interview so that complete and accurate information is obtained
    D. patiently listen to W since rambling is W's style and it cannot be changed

24. Assume that you are interviewing a client. Of the following, the BEST procedure for you to follow in regard to the use of your notebook is to

    A. take out your notebook at the start of the interview and immediately begin taking notes
    B. memorize the important facts related during the interview and enter them after the interview has been completed
    C. advise the client that all his answers are being taken down to insure that he will tell the truth
    D. establish rapport with the client and ask permission to jot down various data in your notebook

25. In order to conduct an effective interview, an interviewer's attention must continuously be directed in two ways, toward himself as well as toward the interviewee. Of the following, the PRIMARY danger in this division of attention is that the

    A. interviewer's behavior may become less natural and thus alienate the interviewee
    B. interviewee's span of attention will be shortened
    C. interviewer's response may be interpreted by the interviewee as being antagonistic
    D. interviewee's more or less concealed prejudices will come to the surface

KEY (CORRECT ANSWERS)

1.	B	11.	C
2.	B	12.	B
3.	B	13.	D
4.	B	14.	D
5.	C	15.	A
6.	D	16.	B
7.	C	17.	C
8.	B	18.	B
9.	D	19.	B
10.	A	20.	B

21. A
22. B
23. C
24. D
25. A

REPORT WRITING
EXAMINATION SECTION
TEST 1

DIRECTIONS: Each question or incomplete statement is followed by several suggested answers or completions. Select the one that BEST answers the question or completes the statement. *PRINT THE LETTER OF THE CORRECT ANSWER IN THE SPACE AT THE RIGHT.*

Questions 1-5.

DIRECTIONS: Questions 1 through 5 are to be answered on the basis of the Report of Offense that appears below.'

REPORT OF OFFENSE	Report No. 26743
	Date of Report 10-12
Inmate *Joseph Brown*	
Age 27	Number *61274*
Sentence *90 days*	Assignment *KU-187*
Place of offense *R.P.W. 4-1*	Date of offense *10/11/*
Offense *Assaulting inmate*	
Details *During 9:00 P.M., cellblock cleanup, inmate John Jones asked for pail being used by Brown. Brown refused. Correction officer requested that Brown comply. Brown then threw pail at Jones with intent to injure him and said he would "get" Jones. Jones not hurt.*	
Force used by officer *None*	
Name of reporting officer *R. Rodriguez*	No. *C-2056*
Name of superior officer *P. Ferguson*	

1. The person who made out this report is
   A. Joseph Brown   B. John Jones
   C. R. Rodriguez   D. P. Ferguson

1.____

2. Disregarding the details, the specific offense reported was
   A. insulting a fellow inmate   B. assaulting a fellow inmate
   C. injuring a fellow inmate   D. disobeying a correct officer

2.____

3. The number of the inmate who committed the offense is
   A. 26743   B. 61274   C. KU-187   D. CJ-2056

3.____

4. The offense took place on
   A. October 11   B. June 12   C. December 10   D. November 13

4.____

5. The place where the offense occurred is identified in the report as
   A. Brown's cell   B. Jones' cell   C. KU-187   D. R.P.W., 4-1

5.____

Questions 6-10.

DIRECTIONS: Questions 6 through 10 are to be answered on the basis of the Report of Loss or Theft that appears below.

REPORT OF LOSS OR THEFT	Date: *12/4*	Time: *9:15 A.M.*
Complaint made by: *Richard Aldridge* *306 S. Walter St.*		☐ Owner ☒ Other – explain: Head of Acctg. Dept.
Type of Property: *Computer*		Value: *$450.00*
Description: *Dell Inspiron laptop*		
Location: *768 N. Margin Ave., Accounting Dept. 3rd Floor*		
Time: *Overnight 12/3 – 12/4*		
Circumstances: *Mr. Aldridge reports he arrived at work 8:45 A.M., found office door open and machine missing. Nothing else reported missing. I investigated and found signs of forced entry; door lock was broken.*		
Signature of Reporting Officer: *B.L. Ramirez*		
Notify: ☐ Building & Grounds Office, 768 N. Margin Ave. ☐ Lost Property Office, 110 Brand Ave. ☒ Security Office, 703 N. Wide Street		

6. The person who made this complaint is
   A. a secretary
   B. a security officer
   C. Richard Aldridge
   D. B.L. Ramirez

7. The report concerns a computer that has been
   A. lost   B. damaged   C. stolen   D. sold

8. The person who took the computer PROBABLY entered the office through
   A. a door
   B. a window
   C. the roof
   D. the basement

9. When did the head of the Accounting Department FIRST notice that the computer was missing?
   A. December 4 at 9:15 A.M.
   B. December 4 at 8:45 A.M.
   C. The night of December 3
   D. The night of December 4

10. The event described in the report took place at
    A. 306 South Walter Street
    B. 768 North Margin Avenue
    C. 110 Brand Avenue
    D. 703 North Wide Street

Questions 11-15.

DIRECTIONS: Questions 11 through 15 are to be answered on the basis of the following excerpt from a recorded Annual Report of the Police Department. This material should be read first and then referred to in answering these questions, which are to be answered SOLELY on the basis of the material herein contained.

LEGAL BUREAU

One of the more important functions of this bureau is to analyze and furnish the department with pertinent information concerning Federal and State statutes and local laws which affect the department, law enforcement or crime prevention. In addition, all measures introduced in the State Legislature and the City Council, which may affect this department, are carefully reviewed by members of the Legal Bureau and, where necessary, opinions and recommendations thereon are prepared.

Another important function of this office is the prosecution of cases in the Magistrate's Courts. This is accomplished by assignment of attorneys who are members of the Legal Bureau to appear in those cases which are deemed to raise issues of importance to the department or questions of law which require technical presentation to facilitate proper determination; and also in those cases where request is made for such appearance by a magistrate, some other official of the city, or a member of the force. Attorneys are regularly assigned to prosecute all cases in the Family Court.

Proposed legislation was prepared and sponsored for introduction in the State Legislature and, at this writing, one of these proposals has already been enacted into law and five others are presently on the Governor's desk awaiting executive action. The new law prohibits the sale or possession of a hypodermic syringe or needle by an unauthorized person. The bureau's proposals awaiting executive action pertain to: an amendment to the Code of Criminal Procedure prohibiting desk officers from taking bail in gambling cases or in cases mentioned in Section 552, Code of Criminal Procedure, including confidence men and swindlers as jostlers in the Penal Law; prohibiting the sale of switch-blade knives of any size to children under 16 and bills extending the licensing period of gunsmiths.

The Legal Bureau has regularly cooperated with the Corporation Counsel and the District attorneys in respect to matters affecting this department, and has continued to advise and represent the Police Athletic League, the Police Sports Association, the Police Relief Fund, and the Police Pension Fund.

The following is a statistical report of the activities of the bureau during the current year as compared with the previous year:

	Current Year	Previous Year
Memoranda of law prepared	68	83
Legal matters forwarded to Corporation Counsel	122	144
Letters requesting legal information	756	807
Letters requesting departmental records	139	111
Matters for publication	17	26
Court appearances of members of bureau	4,678	4,621
Conferences	94	103
Lectures at Police Academy	30	33
Reports on proposed legislation	194	255
Deciphering of codes	79	27
Expert testimony	31	16
Notices to court witnesses	55	81
Briefs prepared	22	18
Court papers prepared	258	—

11. One of the functions of the Legal Bureau is to
    A. review and make recommendations on proposed federal laws affecting law enforcement
    B. prepare opinions on all measures introduced in the state legislature and the City Council
    C. furnish the Police Department with pertinent information concerning all new federal and state laws
    D. analyze all laws affecting the work of the Police Department

12. The Legal Bureau sponsored a bill that would
    A. extend the licenses of gunsmiths
    B. prohibit the sale of switch-blade knives to children of any size
    C. place confidence men and swindlers in the same category as jostlers in the Penal Law
    D. prohibit desk officers from admitting gamblers, confidence men, and swindlers to bail

13. From the report, it is NOT reasonable to infer that
    A. fewer bills affecting the Police Department were introduced in the current year
    B. the preparation of court papers was a new activity assumed in the current year
    C. the Code of Criminal Procedure authorizes desk officers to accept bail in certain cases
    D. the penalty for jostling and swindling is the same

14. According to the statistical report, the activity showing the GREATEST percentage of decrease in the current year compared with the previous year was
    A. matters for publication
    B. reports on proposed legislation
    C. notices to court witnesses
    D. memoranda of law prepared

15. According to the report, the percentage of bills prepared and sponsored by the Legal Bureau, which were passed by the State Legislature and sent to the Governor for approval, was
    A. approximately 3.2%
    B. approximately 2.6%
    C. approximately .5%
    D. not capable of determination from the data given

15.____

KEY (CORRECT ANSWERS)

1.	C	6.	C	11.	D
2.	B	7.	C	12.	C
3.	B	8.	A	13.	D
4.	A	9.	B	14.	A
5.	D	10.	B	15.	D

TEST 2

DIRECTIONS: Each question or incomplete statement is followed by several suggested answers or completions. Select the one that BEST answers the question or completes the statement. *PRINT THE LETTER OF THE CORRECT ANSWER IN THE SPACE AT THE RIGHT.*

Questions 1-2.

DIRECTIONS: Questions 1 and 2 are to be answered on the basis of the Instructions, the Bridge and Tunnel Officer's Toll Report form, and the situation given below. The questions ask how the report form should be filled in based on the Instructions and the information given in the situation.

INSTRUCTIONS

Assume that a Bridge and Tunnel Officer on duty in a toll booth must make an entry on the following report form immediately after each incident in which a vehicle driver does not pay the correct toll.

BRIDGE AND TUNNEL OFFICER'S TOLL REPORT			
Officer_____		Date_____	
Time	Type of Vehicle	Toll Collected	Explanation of Entry
1._____	_____	_____	_____
2._____	_____	_____	_____
_____	_____	_____	_____

SITUATION

John McDonald is a Bridge and Tunnel Officer assigned to toll booth 4, between the hours of 11 P.M. and 1 A.M.. On this particular tour, two incidents occurred. At 11:43 P.M., a five-axle truck stopped at the toll booth and Officer McDonald collected a $2.50 toll from the driver. As the truck passed, he realized the toll should have been $3.30, and he quickly copied the vehicle's license plate number as M724HJ. At 12:35 A.M., a motorcycle went through toll lane 4 without paying the toll. The motorcycle did not have any license plate.

1. The entry which should be made on line1 in the second column is 1.____
   A. 11:43 P.M.
   B. 12:34 A.M.
   C. five-axle truck
   D. motorcycle

2. The above passage does NOT provide the information necessary to fill in which of the following items? 2.____
   A. Officer
   B. Date
   C. Line 1, Toll Collected
   D. Line 2, Time

2 (#2)

FACT SITUATION

Peter Miller is a Correction Officer assigned to duty in Cell-block A. His superior officer is John Doakes. Miller was on duty at 1:30 P.M. on March 21 when he heard a scream for help from Cell 12. He hurried to Cell 12 and found inmate Richard Rogers stamping out a flaming book of matches. Inmate John Jones was screaming. It seems that Jones had accidentally set fire to the entire book of matches while lighting a cigarette, and he had burned his left hand. Smoking was permitted at this hour. Miller reported the incident by phone, and Jones was escorted to the dispensary where his hand was treated at 2:00 P.M. by Dr. Albert Lorillo. Dr. Lorillo determined that Jones could return to his cellblock, but that he should be released from work for four days. The doctor scheduled a re-examination for March 22. A routine investigation of the incident was made by James Lopez. Jones confirmed to this officer that the above statement of the situation was correct,

REPORT OF INMATE INJURY	
(1) Name of Inmate	(2) Assignment
(3) Number	(4) Location
(5) Nature of Injury	(6) Date
(7) Details (how, when, where injury was incurred)	
(8) Received medical attention: date _____ time _____	
(9) Treatment	
(10) Disposition (check one or more): ____ (10-1) Return to housing area ____ (10-2) Return to duty ____ (10-3) Work release ____ days ____ (10-4) Re-examine in ____ days	
(11) Employee reporting injury_____	
(12) Employee's supervisor or superior officer_____	
(13) Medical officer treating injury_____	
(14) Investigating officer_____	
(15) Head of institution_____	

3. Which of the following should be entered in Item 1? 3.____
   A. Peter Miller   B. John Doakes
   C. Richard Rogers   D. John Jones

4. Which of the following should be entered in Item 11? 4.____
   A. Peter Miller   C. James Lopez
   C. Richard Rogers   D. John Jones

5. Which of the following should be entered in Item 8? 5.____
   A. 2/21, 1:30 P.M.   B. 2/21, 2:00 P.M.
   C. 3/21, 1:30 P.M.   D. 3/21, 2:00 P.M.

6. For Item 10, which of the following should be checked? 6.____
   A. 10-4 only   B. 10-1 and 10-4
   C. 10-1, 10-3, and 10-4   D. 10-2, 10-4, and 10-4

3 (#2)

7. Of the following items, which one CANNOT be filled in on the basis of the information given in the Fact Situation? Item   7._____
    A. 12   B. 13   C. 14   D. 15

Questions 8-11.

DIRECTIONS: Questions 8 through 11 are to be answered on the basis of the Fact Situation and the Traffic Control Report form below. Read the Fact Situation carefully, and examine the blank report form. The questions ask how the report form should be filled in based on the information given in the Fact Situation.

FACT SITUATION

Mary Fields is a Traffic Control Agent. Her City Employee Number is Z90019. She is assigned to duty at the intersection of Silver Street and Amber Avenue. On the morning of May 15, she arrives at this intersection at 9:00 A.M. and sees that there is a new *patch job* on the surface of Amber Avenue in the middle of the pedestrian crosswalk and near the northwest corner of the intersection. They day before, an emergency crew was digging here. The hole is now closed and resurfaced, but the patch job on the surface was not done very well. The patch is nearly an inch higher than the surrounding surface, and it has a sharp edge that pedestrians are likely to trip on. Mary Fields thinks this condition is dangerous, and she reports it on the Traffic Control Report form.

TRAFFIC CONTROL REPORT
DEFECTIVE EQUIPMENT OR UNSAFE CONDITION

1. Date of observation _____ 2. Time_____
3. Exact location_____
4. Type of equipment or condition found to be defective or unsafe_____
5. Type of defect_____
6. Name of reporting Agent_____
7. Employee No._____ 8. Precinct No._____

---

8. Which of the following should be entered in Blank 3?   8._____
    A. Silver Street at Amber Avenue, near northwest corner
    B. Silver Street at Amber Avenue, near northwest corner
    C. Amber Avenue at Silver Street, near northeast corner
    D. Amber Avenue at Silver Street, near northwest corner

9. Which of the following should be entered in Blank 4?   9._____
    A. Pedestrian traffic signals
    B. Pedestrian crosswalk markings
    C. Surface patch
    C. Unsafe condition

10. The information called for in Blank 5 is needed to determine what kind of repairs must be made and what kind of repair crew must be sent.
Which of the following entries for Blank 5 will be MOST useful to the people who receive this report in deciding what kind of repair crew to assign to the job?
    A. Pedestrians may stumble and fall.
    B. New patch is higher than rest of surface.
    C. Emergency crew dug a hole here.
    D. Street repairs were not done very well.

10.____

11. There is one blank on the form for which the Fact Situation does not provide the information needed.
The blank that CANNOT be filled out on the basis of the information given is Blank
    A. 2   B. 6   C. 7   D. 8

11.____

Questions 12-15.

DIRECTIONS: Questions 12 through 15 are to be answered on the basis of the Fact Situation and the Report of Arrest form below. Questions ask how the report form should be filled in based on the information given in the Fact Situation.

FACT SITUATION

Jesse Stein is a special officer (security officer) who is assigned to a welfare center at 435 East Smythe Street, Brooklyn. He was on duty there Thursday morning, February 1. At 10:30 A.M., a client named Jo Ann Jones, 40 years old, arrived with her 10-year-old son Peter. Another client, Mary Alice Wiell, 45 years old, immediately began to insult Mrs Jones. When Mrs. Jones told her to go away, Mrs. Wiell pulled out a long knife. The special officer (security officer) intervened and requested Mrs. Wiell to drop the knife. She would not, and he had to use necessary force to disarm her. He arrested her on charges of disorderly conduct, harassment, and possession of a dangerous weapon. Mrs. Wiell lives at 118 Healy Street, Brooklyn, Apartment 4F, and she is unemployed. The reason for her aggressive behavior is not known.

REPORT OF ARREST	
(01)	(08)
(Prisoner's surname)(first)(initial)	(Precinct)
(02)	(09)
(Address)	(Date of Arrest – Month, Day)
(03) (04) (05)	(10)
(Date of Birth) (Age) (Sex)	(Time of arrest)
(06) (07)	(11)
(Occupation) (Where employed)	(Place of arrest)
(12)	
(Specific offenses)	
(13)	(14)
(Arresting officer)	(14) Officer's No.)

12. What entry should be made in Blank 01?   12._____
    A. Jo Ann Jones   B. Jones, Jo Ann
    C. Mary Wiell   D. Wiell, Mary A.

13. Which of the following should be entered in Blank 04?   13._____
    A. 40   B. 40's   C. 45   D. Middle-aged

14. Which of the following should be entered in Blank 09?   14._____
    A. Wednesday, February 1, 10:30 A.M.
    B. February 1
    C. Thursday morning, February 2
    D. Morning, February 4

15. Of the following, which would be the BEST entry to make in Blank 11?   15._____
    A. Really Street Welfare Center   B. Brooklyn
    C. 435 e. Smythe St., Brooklyn   D. 118 Heally St., Apt. 4F

KEY (CORRECT ANSWERS)

1. C	6. C	11. D
2. B	7. D	12. D
3. D	8. D	13. C
4. A	9. C	14. B
5. D	10. B	15. C

PREPARING WRITTEN MATERIALS
EXAMINATION SECTION
TEST 1

DIRECTIONS: Each question consists of a sentence which may be classified appropriately under one of the following four categories:
- A. Incorrect because of faulty grammar or sentence structure.
- B. Incorrect because of faulty punctuation.
- C. Incorrect because of faulty spelling or capitalization.
- D. Correct

Examine each sentence carefully. Then, in the space at the right, print the capital letter preceding the option which is the BEST of the four suggested above. All incorrect sentences contain only one type of error. Consider a sentence correct if it contains none of the types of errors mentioned, although there may be other correct ways of expressing the same thought.

1. The fire apparently started in the storeroom, which is usually locked. 1._____
2. On approaching the victim two bruises were noticed by this officer. 2._____
3. The officer, who was there examined the report with great care. 3._____
4. Each employee in the office had a separate desk. 4._____
5. The suggested procedure is similar to the one now in use. 5._____
6. No one was more pleased with the new procedure than the chauffeur. 6._____
7. He tried to pursuade her to change the procedure. 7._____
8. The total of the expenses charged to petty cash were high. 8._____
9. An understanding between him and I was finally reached. 9._____
10. It was at the supervisor's request that the clerk agreed to postpone his vacation. 10._____
11. We do not believe that it is necessary for both he and the clerk to attend the conference. 11._____
12. All employees, who display perseverance, will be given adequate recognition. 12._____
13. He regrets that some of us employees are dissatisfied with our new assignments. 13._____

14. "Do you think that the raise was merited," asked the supervisor? 14._____

15. The new manual of procedure is a valuable supplament to our rules and regulation. 15._____

16. The typist admitted that she had attempted to pursuade the other employees to assist her in her work. 16._____

17. The supervisor asked that all amendments to the regulations be handled by you and I. 17._____

18. They told both he and I that the prisoner had escaped. 18._____

19. Any superior officer, who, disregards the just complaints of his subordinates, is remiss in the performance of his duty. 19._____

20. Only those members of the national organization who resided in the Middle west attended the conference in Chicago. 20._____

21. We told him to give the investigation assignment to whoever was available. 21._____

22. Please do not disappoint and embarass us by not appearing in court. 22._____

23. Despite the efforts of the Supervising mechanic, the elevator could not be started. 23._____

24. The U.S. Weather Bureau, weather record for the accident date was checked. 24._____

KEY (CORRECT ANSWERS)

1.	D	11.	A
2.	A	12.	B
3.	B	13.	D
4.	D	14.	B
5.	D	15.	C
6.	D	16.	C
7.	C	17.	A
8.	A	18.	A
9.	A	19.	B
10.	D	20.	C

21.	D
22.	C
23.	C
24.	B

TEST 2

DIRECTIONS: Each question consists of a sentence. Some of the sentences contain errors in English grammar or usage, punctuation, spelling, or capitalization. A sentence does not contain an error simply because it could be written in a different manner. Choose answer:
- A. If the sentence contains an error in English grammar or usage.
- B. if the sentence contains an error in punctuation.
- C. If the sentence contains an error in spelling or capitalization
- D. If the sentence does not contain any errors.

1. The severity of the sentence prescribed by contemporary statutes—including both the former and the revised New York Penal Laws—do not depend on what crime was intended by the offender. 1.____

2. It is generally recognized that two defects in the early law of attempt played a part in the birth of burglary: (1) immunity from prosecution for conduct short of the last act before completion of the crime, and (2) the relatively minor penalty imposed for an attempt (it being a common law misdemeanor) vis-à-vis the completed offense. 2.____

3. The first sentence of the statute is applicable to employees who enter their place of employment, invited guests, and all other persons who have an express or implied license or privilege to enter the premises. 3.____

4. Contemporary criminal codes in the United States generally divide burglary into various degrees, differentiating the categories according to place, time and other attendent circumstances. 4.____

5. The assignment was completed in record time but the payroll for it has not yet been prepaid. 5.____

6. The operator, on the other hand, is willing to learn me how to use the mimeograph. 6.____

7. She is the prettiest of the three sisters. 7.____

8. She doesn't know; if the mail has arrived. 8.____

9. The doorknob of the office door is broke. 9.____

10. Although the department's supply of scratch pads and stationery have diminished considerably, the allotment for our division has not been reduced. 10.____

11. You have not told us whom you wish to designate as your secretary. 11.____

12. Upon reading the minutes of the last meeting, the new proposal was taken up for consideration. 12.____

13. Before beginning the discussion, we locked the door as a precautionery measure.   13.____

14. The supervisor remarked, "Only those clerks, who perform routine work, are permitted to take a rest period."   14.____

15. Not only will this duplicating machine make accurate copies, but it will also produce a quantity of work equal to fifteen transcribing typists.   15.____

16. "Mr. Jones," said the supervisor, "we regret our inability to grant you an extention of your leave of absence."   16.____

17. Although the employees find the work monotonous and fatigueing, they rarely complain.   17.____

18. We completed the tabulation of the receipts on time despite the fact that Miss Smith our fastest operator was absent for over a week.   18.____

19. The reaction of the employees who attended the meeting, as well as the reaction of those who did not attend, indicates clearly that the schedule is satisfactory to everyone concerned.   19.____

20. Of the two employees, the one in our office is the most efficient.   20.____

21. No one can apply or even understand, the new rules and regulations.   21.____

22. A large amount of supplies were stored in the empty office.   22.____

23. If an employee is occassionally asked to work overtime, he should do so willingly.   23.____

24. It is true that the new procedures are difficult to use but, we are certain that you will learn them quickly.   24.____

25. The office manager said that he did not know who would be given a large allotment under the new plan.   25.____

KEY (CORRECT ANSWERS)

1. A
2. D
3. D
4. C
5. C

6. A
7. D
8. B
9. A
10. A

11. D
12. A
13. C
14. B
15. A

16. C
17. C
18. B
19. D
20. A

21. B
22. A
23. C
24. B
25. D

TEST 3

DIRECTIONS: Each of the following sentences may be classified MOST appropriately under one of the following categories:
   A. Faulty because of incorrect grammar
   B. Faulty because of incorrect punctuation
   C. Faulty because of incorrect capitalization
   D. Correct

Examine each sentence carefully. Then, in the space at the right, print the capital letter preceding the option which is the BEST of the four suggested above. All incorrect sentence contain but one type of error. Consider a sentence correct if it contains none of the types of errors mentioned, even though there may be other correct ways of expressing the same thought.

1. The desk, as well as the chairs, were moved out of the office. 1.____

2. The clerk whose production was greatest for the month won a day's vacation as first prize. 2.____

3. Upon entering the room, the employees were found hard at work at their desks. 3.____

4. John Smith our new employee always arrives at work on time. 4.____

5. Punish whoever is guilty of stealing the money. 5.____

6. Intelligent and persistent effort lead to success no matter what the job may be. 6.____

7. The secretary asked, "can you call again at three o'clock?" 7.____

8. He told us, that if the report was not accepted at the next meeting, it would have to be rewritten. 8.____

9. He would not have sent the letter if he had known that it would cause so much excitement. 9.____

10. We all looked forward to him coming to visit us. 10.____

11. If you find that you are unable to complete the assignment please notify me as soon as possible. 11.____

12. Every girl in the office went home on time but me; there was still some work for me to finish. 12.____

13. He wanted to know who the letter was addressed to, Mr. Brown or Mr. Smith. 13.____

14. "Mr. Jones, he said, please answer this letter as soon as possible." 14.____

15. The new clerk had an unusual accent inasmuch as he was born and educated in the south. 15.____

16. Although he is younger than her, he earns a higher salary. 16.____

17. Neither of the two administrators are going to attend the conference being held in Washington, D.C. 17.____

18. Since Miss Smith and Miss Jones have more experience than us, they have been given more responsible duties. 18.____

19. Mr. Shaw the supervisor of the stock room maintains an inventory of stationery and office supplies. 19.____

20. Inasmuch as this matter affects both you and I, we should take joint action. 20.____

21. Who do you think will be able to perform this highly technical work? 21.____

22. Of the two employees, John is considered the most competent. 22.____

23. He is not coming home on tuesday; we expect him next week. 23.____

24. Stenographers, as well as typists must be able to type rapidly and accurately. 24.____

25. Having been placed in the safe we were sure that the money would not be stolen. 25.____

KEY (CORRECT ANSWERS)

1.	A		11.	B
2.	D		12.	D
3.	A		13.	A
4.	B		14.	B
5.	D		15.	C
6.	A		16.	A
7.	C		17.	A
8.	B		18.	A
9.	D		19.	B
10.	A		20.	A

21. D
22. A
23. C
24. B
25. A

TEST 4

DIRECTIONS: Each of the following sentences consist of four sentences lettered A, B, C, and D. One of the sentences in each group contains an error in grammar or punctuation. Indicate the INCORRECT sentence in each group. *PRINT THE LETTER OF THE CORRECT ANSWER IN THE SPACE AT THE RIGHT.*

1. A. Give the message to whoever is on duty.
   B. The teacher who's pupil won first prize presented the award.
   C. Between you and me, I don't expect the program to succeed.
   D. His running to catch the bus caused the accident.

   1.____

2. A. The process, which was patented only last year is already obsolete.
   B. His interest in science (which continues to the present) led him to convert his basement into a laboratory.
   C. He described the book as "verbose, repetitious, and bombastic".
   D. Our new director will need to possess three qualities: vision, patience, and fortitude.

   2.____

3. A. The length of ladder trucks varies considerably.
   B. The probationary fireman reported to the officer to who he was assigned.
   C. The lecturer emphasized the need for we firemen to be punctual.
   D. Neither the officers nor the members of the company knew about the new procedure.

   3.____

4. A. Ham and eggs is the specialty of the house.
   B. He is one of the students who are on probation.
   C. Do you think that either one of us have a chance to be nominated for president of the class?
   D. I assume that either he was to be in charge or you were.

   4.____

5. A. Its a long road that has no turn.
   B. To run is more tiring than to walk.
   C. We have been assigned three new reports: namely, the statistical summary, the narrative summary, and the budgetary summary.
   D. Had the first payment been made in January, the second would be due in April.

   5.____

6. A. Each employer has his own responsibilities.
   B. If a person speaks correctly, they make a good impression.
   C. Every one of the operators has had her vacation.
   D. Has anybody filed his report?

   6.____

7. A. The manager, with all his salesmen, was obliged to go.
   B. Who besides them is to sign the agreement?
   C. One report without the others is incomplete.
   D. Several clerks, as well as the proprietor, was injured.

   7.____

2 (#4)

8. A. A suspension of these activities is expected.
    B. The machine is economical because first cost and upkeep are low.
    C. A knowledge of stenography and filing are required for this position.
    D. The condition in which the goods were received shows that the packing was not done properly.

8.____

9. A. There seems to be a great many reasons for disagreement.
    B. It does not seem possible that they could have failed.
    C. Have there always been too few applicants for these positions?
    D. There is no excuse for these errors.

9.____

10. A. We shall be pleased to answer your question.
    B. Shall we plan the meeting for Saturday?
    C. I will call you promptly at seven.
    D. Can I borrow your book after you have read it?

10.____

11. A. You are as capable as I.
    B. Everyone is willing to sign but him and me.
    C. As for he and his assistant, I cannot praise them too highly.
    D. Between you and me, I think he will be dismissed.

11.____

12. A. Our competitors bid above us last week.
    B. The survey which was began last year has not yet been completed.
    C. The operators had shown that they understood their instructions.
    D. We have never ridden over worse roads.

12.____

13. A. Who did they say was responsible?
    B. Whom did you suspect?
    C. Who do you suppose it was?
    D. Whom do you mean?

13.____

14. A. Of the two propositions, this is the worse.
    B. Which report do you consider the best—the one in January or the one in July?
    C. I believe this is the most practicable of the many plans submitted.
    D. He is the youngest employee in the organization.

14.____

15. A. The firm had but three orders last week.
    B. That doesn't really seem possible.
    C. After twenty years scarcely none of the old business remains.
    D. Has he done nothing about it?

15.____

KEY (CORRECT ANSWERS)

1. B
2. A
3. C
4. C
5. A
6. B
7. D
8. C
9. A
10. D
11. C
12. B
13. A
14. B
15. C

PREPARING WRITTEN MATERIAL
EXAMINATION SECTION
TEST 1

DIRECTIONS: Each question or incomplete statement is followed by several suggested answers or completions. Select the one that BEST answers the question or completes the statement. *PRINT THE LETTER OF THE CORRECT ANSWER IN THE SPACE AT THE RIGHT.*

Questions 1-4.

DIRECTIONS: Questions 1 through 4 each consist of a sentence which may or may not be an example of good English. The underlined parts of each sentence may be correct or incorrect. Examine each sentence, considering grammar, punctuation, spelling, and capitalization. If the English usage in the underlined parts of the sentence given is better than any of the changes in the underlined words suggested in options B, C, or D, choose option A. If the changes in the underlined words suggested in options B, C, or D would make the sentence correct, choose the correct option. Do not choose an option that will change the meaning of the sentence.

1. This Fall, the office will be closed on Columbus Day, October 9th. 1.____
   A. Correct as is
   B. fall...Columbus Day; October
   C. Fall...columbus day, October
   D. fall...Columbus Day – October

2. There weren't no paper in the supply closet. 2.____
   A. Correct as is
   B. weren't any
   C. wasn't any
   D. wasn't no

3. The alphabet, or A to Z sequence are the basis of most filing systems. 3.____
   A. Correct as is
   B. alphabet, or A to Z sequence, is
   C. alphabet, or A to Z sequence, are
   D. alphabet, or A too Z sequence, is

4. The Office Aide checked the register and finding the date of the meeting. 4.____
   A. Correct as is
   B. regaster and finding
   C. register and found
   D. regaster and found

Questions 5-10.

DIRECTIONS: Questions 5 through 10 consist of sentences which contain examples of correct or incorrect English usage. Examine each sentence with reference to grammar, spelling, punctuation, and capitalization. Chooses one of the following options that would be BEST for correct English usage:

89

2 (#1)

    A. The sentence is correct
    B. There is one mistake
    C. There are two mistakes
    D. There are three mistakes

5. Mrs. Fitzgerald came to the 59th Precinct to retreive her property which were stolen earlier in the week.   5._____

6. The two officer's responded to the call, only to find that the perpatrator and the victim have left the scene.   6._____

7. Mr. Coleman called the 61st Precinct to report that, upon arriving at his store, he discovered that there was a large hole in the wall and that three boxes of radios were missing.   7._____

8. The Administrative Leiutenant of the 62nd Precinct held a meeting which was attended by all the civilians, assigned to the Precinct.   8._____

9. Three days after the robbery occurred the detective apprahended two suspects and recovered the stolen items.   9._____

10. The Community Affairs Officer of the 64th Precinct is the liaison between the Precinct and the community; he works closely with various community organizations, and elected officials,   10._____

Questions 11-18.

DIRECTIONS: Questions 11 through 18 are to be answered on the basis of the following paragraph, which contains some deliberate errors in spelling and/or grammar and/or punctuation. Each line of the paragraph is preceded by a number. There are 9 lines and 9 numbers.

Line No.	Paragraph Line
1	The protection of life and proporty are, one of
2	the oldest and most important functions of a city.
3	New York City has it's own full-time police Agency.
4	The police Department has the power an it shall
5	be there duty to preserve the Public piece,
6	prevent crime detect and arrest offenders, supress
7	riots, protect the rites of persons and property, etc.
8	The maintainance of sound relations with the community they
9	serve is an important function of law enforcement officers

11. How many errors are contained in line one?   11._____

12. How many errors are contained in line two?   12._____

13. How many errors are contained in line three?   13._____

14. How many errors are contained in line four? 14._____

15. How many errors are contained in line five? 15._____

16. How many errors are contained in line six? 16._____

17. How many errors are contained in line seven? 17._____

18. How many errors are contained in line eight? 18._____

19. In the sentence, *The candidate wants to file his application for preference before it is too late*, the word *before* is used as a(n) 19._____
    A. preposition
    B. subordinating conjunction
    C. pronoun
    D. adverb

20. The one of the following sentences which is grammatically PREFERABLE to the others is: 20._____
    A. Our engineers will go over your blueprints so that you may have no problems in construction.
    B. For a long time he had been arguing that we, not he, are to blame for the confusion.
    C. I worked on this automobile for two hours and still cannot find out what is wrong with it.
    D. Accustomed to all kinds of hardships, fatigue seldom bothers veteran policemen.

KEY (CORRECT ANSWERS)

1.	A	11.	C
2.	C	12.	D
3.	B	13.	C
4.	C	14.	B
5.	C	15.	C
6.	D	16.	B
7.	A	17.	A
8.	C	18.	A
9.	C	19.	B
10.	B	20.	A

TEST 2

DIRECTIONS: Each question or incomplete statement is followed by several suggested answers or completions. Select the one that BEST answers the question or completes the statement. *PRINT THE LETTER OF THE CORRECT ANSWER IN THE SPACE AT THE RIGHT.*

1. The plural of   1.____
   A. turkey is turkies
   B. cargo is cargoes
   C. bankruptcy is bankruptcys
   D. son-in-law is son-in-laws

2. The abbreviation *viz.* means MOST NEARLY   2.____
   A. namely   B. for example   C. the following   D. see

3. In the sentence, *A man in a light-grey suit waited thirty-five minutes in the ante-room for the all-important document,* the word IMPROPERLY hyphenated is   3.____
   A. light-grey   B. thirty-five   C. ante-room   D. all-important

4. The MOST accurate of the following sentences is: 4.____
   A. The commissioner, as well as his deputy and various bureau heads, were present.
   B. A new organization of employers and employees have been formed.
   C. One or the other of these men have been selected.
   D. The number of pages in the book is enough to discourage a reader.

5. The MOST accurate of the following sentences is: 5.____
   A. Between you and me, I think he is the better man.
   B. He was believed to be me.
   C. Is it us that you wish to see?
   D. The winners are him and her.

Questions 6-13.

DIRECTIONS: The sentences numbered 6 through 13 deal with some phase of police activity. They may be classified most appropriately under one of the following four categories.

   A. Faulty because of incorrect grammar
   B. Faulty because of incorrect punctuation
   C. Faulty because of incorrect use of a word
   D. Correct

Examine each sentence carefully. Then, in the space at the right, print the capital letter preceding the option which is the BEST of the four suggested above. All incorrect sentences contain only one type of error. Consider a sentence correct if it contains none of the types of errors mentioned, even though there may be other correct ways of expressing the same thought.

2 (#2)

6. The Department Medal of Honor is awarded to a member of the Police Force who distinguishes himself inconspicuously in the line of police duty by the performance of an act of gallantry.

6.____

7. Members of the Detective Division are charged with the prevention of crime, the detection and arrest of criminals and the recovery of lost or stolen property,

7.____

8. Detectives are selected from the uniformed patrol forces after they have indicated by conduct, aptitude and performance that they are qualified for the more intricate duties of a detective.

8.____

9. The patrolman, pursuing his assailant, exchanged shots with the gunman and immortally wounded him as he fled into a nearby building.

9.____

10. The members of the Traffic Division has to enforce the Vehicle and Traffic Law, the Traffic Regulations and ordinances relating to vehicular and pedestrian traffic.

10.____

11. After firing a shot at the gunman, the crowd dispersed from the patrolman's line of fire.

11.____

12. The efficiency of the Missing Persons Bureau is maintained with a maximum of public personnel due to the specialized training given to its members.

12.____

13. Records of persons arrested for violations of Vehicle and Traffic Regulations are transmitted upon request to precincts, courts and other authorized agencies.

13.____

14. Following are two sentences which may or may not be written in correct English:
    I. Two clients assaulted the officer.
    II. The van is illegally parked.
    Which one of the following statements is CORRECT?
    A. Only Sentence I is written in correct English.
    B. Only Sentence II is written in correct English.
    C. Sentences I and II are both written in correct English.
    D. Neither Sentence I nor Sentence II is written in correct English.

14.____

15. Following are two sentences which may or may not be written in correct English:
    I. Security Officer Rollo escorted the visitor to the patrolroom.
    II. Two entry were made in the facility logbook.
    Which one of the following statements is CORRECT?
    A. Only Sentence I is written in correct English.
    B. Only Sentence II is written in correct English.
    C. Sentences I and II are both written in correct English.
    D. Neither Sentence I nor Sentence II is written in correct English.

15.____

16. Following are two sentences which may or may not be written in correct English: 16.____
    I. Officer McElroy putted out a small fire in the wastepaper basket.
    II. Special Officer Janssen told the visitor where he could obtained a pass.
    Which one of the following statements is CORRECT?
    A. Only Sentence I is written in correct English.
    B. Only Sentence II is written in correct English.
    C. Sentences I and II are both written in correct English.
    D. Neither Sentence I nor Sentence II is written in correct English.

17. Following are two sentences which may or may not be written in correct English: 17.____
    I. Security Officer Warren observed a broken window while he was on his post in Hallway C.
    II. The worker reported that two typewriters had been stolen from the office,
    Which one of the following statements is CORRECT?
    A. Only Sentence I is written in correct English.
    B. Only Sentence II is written in correct English.
    C. Sentences I and II are both written in correct English.
    D. Neither Sentence I nor Sentence II is written in correct English,

18. Following are two sentences which may or may not be written in correct English: 18.____
    I. Special Officer Cleveland was attempting to calm an emotionally disturbed visitor.
    II. The visitor did not stop crying and calling for his wife.
    Which one of the following statements is CORRECT?
    A. Only Sentence I is written in correct English.
    B. Only Sentence II is written in correct English.
    C. Sentences I and II are both written in correct English.
    D. Neither Sentence I nor Sentence II is written in correct English.

19. Following are two sentences that may or may not be written in correct English: 19.____
    I. While on patrol, I observes a vagrant loitering near the drug dispensary.
    II. I escorted the vagrant out of the building and off the premises.
    Which one of the following statements is CORRECT?
    A. Only Sentence I is written in correct English.
    B. Only Sentence II is written in correct English.
    C. Sentences I and II are both written in correct English.
    D. Neither Sentence I nor Sentence II is written in correct English.

20. Following are two sentences which may or may not be written in correct English: 20.____
    I. At 4:00 P.M., Sergeant Raymond told me to evacuate the waiting area immediately due to a bomb threat.
    II. Some of the clients did not want to leave the building.
    Which one of the following statements is CORRECT?
    A. Only Sentence I is written in correct English.
    B. Only Sentence II is written in correct English.
    C. Sentences I and II are both written in correct English.
    D. Neither Sentence I nor Sentence II is written in correct English.

KEY (CORRECT ANSWERS)

1.	B	11.	A
2.	A	12.	C
3.	C	13.	D
4.	D	14.	C
5.	A	15.	A
6.	C	16.	D
7.	B	17.	A
8.	D	18.	A
9.	C	19.	B
10.	A	20.	C

PREPARING WRITTEN MATERIAL
EXAMINATION SECTION
TEST 1

DIRECTIONS: Each question or incomplete statement is followed by several suggested answers or completions. Select the one that BEST answers the question or completes the statement. *PRINT THE LETTER OF THE CORRECT ANSWER IN THE SPACE AT THE RIGHT.*

1. The one of the following sentences which is LEAST acceptable from the viewpoint of correct usage is:
   A. The police thought the fugitive to be him.
   B. The criminals set a trap for whoever would fall into it.
   C. It is ten years ago since the fugitive fled from the city.
   D. The lecturer argued that criminals are usually cowards.
   E. The police removed four bucketfuls of earth from the scene of the crime.

1.____

2. The one of the following sentences which is LEAST acceptable from the viewpoint of correct usage is:
   A. The patrolman scrutinized the report with great care.
   B. Approaching the victim of the assault, two bruises were noticed by the patrolman.
   C. As soon as I had broken down the door, I stepped into the room.
   D. I observed the accused loitering near the building, which was closed at the time.
   E. The storekeeper complained that his neighbor was guilty of violating a local ordinance.

2.____

3. The one of the following sentences which is LEAST acceptable from the viewpoint of correct usage is:
   A. I realized immediately that he intended to assault the woman, so I disarmed him.
   B. It was apparent that Mr. Smith's explanation contained many inconsistencies.
   C. Despite the slippery condition of the street, he managed to stop the vehicle before injuring the child.
   D. Not a single one of them wish, despite the damage to property, to make a formal complaint.
   E. The body was found lying on the floor.

3.____

4. The one of the following sentences which contains NO error in usage is:
   A. After the robbers left, the proprietor stood tied in his chair for about two hours before help arrived.
   B. In the cellar I found the watchman's hat and coat.
   C. The persons living in adjacent apartments stated that they had heard no unusual noises.

4.____

D. Neither a knife or any firearms were found in the room.
E. Walking down the street, the shouting of the crowd indicated that something was wrong.

5. The one of the following sentences which contains NO error in usage is:
   A. The policeman lay a firm hand on the suspect's shoulder.
   B. It is true that neither strength nor agility are the most important requirement for a good patrolman.
   C. Good citizens constantly strive to do more than merely comply the restraints imposed by society.
   D. No decision was made as to whom the prize should be awarded.
   E. Twenty years is considered a severe sentence for a felony.

6. Which of the following sentences is NOT expressed in standard English usage?
   A. The victim reached a pay-phone booth and manages to call police headquarters.
   B. By the time the call was received, the assailant had left the scene.
   C. The victim has been a respected member of the community for the past eleven years.
   D. Although the lighting was bad and the shadows were deep, the storekeeper caught sight of the attacker.
   E. Additional street lights have since been installed, and the patrols have been strengthened.

7. Which of the following sentences is NOT expressed in standard English usage?
   A. The judge upheld the attorney's right to question the witness about the missing glove.
   B. To be absolutely fair to all parties is the jury's chief responsibility.
   C. Having finished the report, a loud noise in the next room startled the sergeant.
   D. The witness obviously enjoyed having played a part in the proceedings.
   E. The sergeant planned to assign the case to whoever arrived first.

8. In which of the following sentences is a word misused?
   A. As a matter of principle, the captain insisted that the suspect's partner be brought for questioning.
   B. The principle suspect had been detained at the station house for most of the day.
   C. The principal in the crime had no previous criminal record, but his closest associate had been convicted of felonies on two occasions.
   D. The interest payments had been made promptly, but the firm had been drawing upon the principal for these payments.
   E. The accused insisted that his high school principal would furnish him a character reference.

9. Which of the following statements is ambiguous?   9._____
   A. Mr. Sullivan explained why Mr. Johnson had been dismissed from his job.
   B. The storekeeper told the patrolman he had made a mistake.
   C. After waiting three hours, the patients in the doctor's office were sent home.
   D. The janitor's duties were to maintain the building in good shape and to answer tenants' complaints.
   E. The speed limit should, in my opinion, be raised to sixty miles an hour on that stretch of road.

10. In which of the following is the punctuation or capitalization faulty?   10._____
    A. The accident occurred at an intersection in the Kew Gardens section of Queens, near the bus stop.
    B. The sedan, not the convertible, was struck in the side.
    C. Before any of the patrolmen had left the police car received an important message from headquarters.
    D. The dog that had been stolen was returned to his master, John Dempsey, who lived in East Village.
    E. The letter had been sent to 12 Hillside Terrace, Rutland, Vermont 05702.

Questions 11-25.

DIRECTIONS: Questions 11 through 25 are to be answered in accordance with correct English usage; that is, standard English rather than nonstandard or substandard. Nonstandard and substandard English includes words or expressions usually classified as slang, dialect, illiterate, etc., which are not generally accepted as correct in current written communication. Standard English also requires clarity, proper punctuation and capitalization and appropriate use of words. Write the letter of the sentence NOT expressed in standard English usage in the space at the right.

11. A. There were three witnesses to the accident.   11._____
    B. At least three witnesses were found to testify for the plaintiff.
    C. Three of the witnesses who took the stand was uncertain about the defendant's competence to drive.
    D. Only three witnesses came forward to testify for the plaintiff.
    E. The three witnesses to the accident were pedestrians.

12. A. The driver had obviously drunk too many martinis before leaving for home.   12._____
    B. The boy who drowned had swum in these same waters many times before.
    C. The petty thief had stolen a bicycle from a private driveway before he was apprehended.
    D. The detectives had brung in the heroin shipment they intercepted.
    E. The passengers had never ridden in a converted bus before.

13. A. Between you and me, the new platoon plan sounds like a good idea. 13.____
     B. Money from an aunt's estate was left to his wife and he.
     C. He and I were assigned to the same patrol for the first time in two months.
     D. Either you or he should check the front door of that store.
     E. The captain himself was not sure of the witness's reliability.

14. A. The alarm had scarcely begun to ring when the explosion occurred. 14.____
     B. Before the firemen arrived at the scene, the second story had been destroyed.
     C. Because of the dense smoke and heat, the firemen could hardly approach the now-blazing structure.
     D. According to the patrolman's report, there wasn't nobody in the store when the explosion occurred.
     E. The sergeant's suggestion was not at all unsound, but no one agreed with him.

15. A. The driver and the passenger they were both found to be intoxicated. 15.____
     B. The driver and the passenger talked slowly and not too clearly.
     C. Neither the driver nor his passengers were able to give a coherent account of the accident.
     D. In a corner of the room sat the passenger, quietly dozing.
     E. the driver finally told a strange and unbelievable story, which the passenger contradicted.

16. A. Under the circumstances I decided not to continue my examination of the premises. 16.____
     B. There are many difficulties now not comparable with those existing in 1960.
     C. Friends of the accused were heard to announce that the witness had better been away on the day of the trial.
     D. The two criminals escaped in the confusion that followed the explosion.
     E. The aged man was struck by the considerateness of the patrolman's offer.

17. A. An assemblage of miscellaneous weapons lay on the table. 17.____
     B. Ample opportunities were given to the defendant to obtain counsel.
     C. The speaker often alluded to his past experience with youthful offenders in the armed forces.
     D. The sudden appearance of the truck aroused my suspicions.
     E. Her studying had a good affect on her grades in high school.

18. A. He sat down in the theater and began to watch the movie. 18.____
     B. The girl had ridden horses since she was four years old.
     C. Application was made on behalf of the prosecutor to cite the witness for contempt.
     D. The bank robber, with his two accomplices, were caught in the act.
     E. His story is simply not credible.

19. A. The angry boy said that he did not like those kind of friends.
    B. The merchant's financial condition was so precarious that he felt he must avail himself of any offer of assistance.
    C. He is apt to promise more than he can perform.
    D. Looking at the messy kitchen, the housewife felt like crying.
    E. A clerk was left in charge of the stolen property.

19.____

20. A. His wounds were aggravated by prolonged exposure to sub-freezing temperatures.
    B. The prosecutor remarked that the witness was not averse to changing his story each time he was interviewed.
    C. The crime pattern indicated that the burglars were adapt in the handling of explosives.
    D. His rigid adherence to a fixed plan brought him into renewed conflict with his subordinates.
    E. He had anticipated that the sentence would be delivered by noon.

20.____

21. A. The whole arraignment procedure is badly in need of revision.
    B. After his glasses were broken in the fight, he would of gone to the optometrist if he could.
    C. Neither Tom nor Jack brought his lunch to work.
    D. He stood aside until the quarrel was over.
    E. A statement in the psychiatrist's report disclosed that the probationer vowed to have his revenge.

21.____

22. A. His fiery and intemperate speech to the striking employees fatally affected any chance of a future reconciliation.
    B. The wording of the statute has been variously construed.
    C. The defendant's attorney, speaking in the courtroom, called the official a demagogue who contemptuously disregarded the judge's orders.
    D. The baseball game is likely to be the most exciting one this year.
    E. The mother divided the cookies among her two children.

22.____

23. A. There was only a bed and a dresser in the dingy room.
    B. John was one of the few students that have protested the new rule.
    C. It cannot be argued that the child's testimony is negligible; it is, on the contrary, of the greatest importance.
    D. The basic criterion for clearance was so general that officials resolved any doubts in favor of dismissal.
    E. Having just returned from a long vacation, the officer found the city unbearably hot.

23.____

24. A. The librarian ought to give more help to small children.
    B. The small boy was criticized by the teacher because he often wrote careless.
    C. It was generally doubted whether the women would permit the use of her apartment for intelligence operations.
    D. The probationer acts differently every time the officer visits him.
    E. Each of the newly appointed officers has 12 years of service.

24.____

25. A. The North is the most industrialized region in the country.
    B. L. Patrick Gray 3d, the bureau's acting director, stated that, while "rehabilitation is fine" for some convicted criminals, "it is a useless gesture for those who resist every such effort."
    C. Careless driving, faulty mechanism, narrow or badly kept roads all play their part in causing accidents.
    D. The childrens' books were left in the bus.
    E. It was a matter of internal security; consequently, he felt no inclination to rescind his previous order.

25.____

KEY (CORRECT ANSWERS)

1.	C	11.	C
2.	B	12.	D
3.	D	13.	B
4.	C	14.	D
5.	E	15.	A
6.	A	16.	C
7.	C	17.	E
8.	B	18.	D
9.	B	19.	A
10.	C	20.	C

21.	B
22.	E
23.	B
24.	B
25.	D

TEST 2

DIRECTIONS: Each question or incomplete statement is followed by several suggested answers or completions. Select the one that BEST answers the question or completes the statement. *PRINT THE LETTER OF THE CORRECT ANSWER IN THE SPACE AT THE RIGHT.*

Questions 1-6.

DIRECTIONS: Each of Questions 1 through 6 consists of a statement which contains a word (one of those underlined) that is either incorrectly used because it is not in keeping with the meaning the quotation is evidently intended to convey, or is misspelled. There is only one INCORRECT word in each quotation. Of the four underlined words, determine if the first one should be replaced by the word lettered A, the second replaced by the word lettered B, the third replaced by the word lettered C, or the fourth replaced by the word lettered D.

1. Whether one depends on fluorescent or artificial light or both, adequate standards should be maintained by means of systematic tests.   1.____
   A. natural   B. safeguards   C. established   D. routine

2. A police officer has to be prepared to assume his knowledge as a social scientist in the community.   2.____
   A. forced   B. role   C. philosopher   D. street

3. It is practically impossible to indicate whether a sentence is too long simply by measuring its length.   3.____
   A. almost   B. tell   C. very   D. guessing

4. Strong leaders are required to organize a community for delinquency prevention and for dissemination of organized crime and drug addiction.   4.____
   A. tactics   B. important   C. control   D. meetings

5. The demonstrators who were taken to the Criminal Courts building in Manhattan (because it was large enough to accommodate them), contended that the arrests were unwarranted.   5.____
   A. demonstraters   B. Manhatten
   C. accomodate   D. unwarranted

6. They were guaranteed a calm atmosphere, free from harassment, which would be conducive to quiet consideration of the indictments.   6.____
   A. guarenteed   B. atmspher
   C. harassment   D. inditements

103

Questions 7-11.

DIRECTIONS: Each of Questions 7 through 11 consists of a statement containing four words in capital letters. One of these words in capital letters is not in keeping with the meaning which the statement is evidently intended to carry. The four words in capital letters in each statement are reprinted after the statement. Print the capital letter preceding the one of the four words which does MOST to spoil the true meaning of the statement in the space at the right.

7. Retirement and pension systems are essential not only to provide employees with with a means of support in the future, but also to prevent longevity and CHARITABLE considerations from UPSETTING the PROMOTIONAL opportunities RETIRED members of the career service.   7.____
   A. charitable   B. upsetting   C. promotional   D. retired

8. Within each major DIVISION in a properly set up public or private organization, provision is made so that each NECESSARY activity is CARED for and lines of authority and responsibility are clear-cut and INFINITE.   8.____
   A. division   B. necessary   C. cared   D. infinite

9. In public service, the scale of salaries paid must be INCIDENTAL to the services rendered, with due CONSIDERATION for the attraction of the desired MANPOWER and for the maintenance of a standard of living COMMENSURATE with the work to be performed.   9.____
   A. incidental   B. consideration
   C. manpower   D. commensurate

10. An understanding of the AIMS of an organization by the staff will AID greatly in increasing the DEMAND of the correspondence work of the office, and will to a large extent DETERMINE the nature of the correspondence.   10.____
   A. aims   B. aid   C. demand   D. determine

11. BECAUSE the Civil Service Commission strongly feels that the MERIT system is a key factor in the MAINTENANCE of democratic government, it has adopted as one of its major DEFENSES the progressive democratization of its own procedures in dealing with candidates for positions in the public service.   11.____
   A. Because   B. merit   C. maintenance   D. defenses

Questions 12-14.

DIRECTIONS: Questions 12 through 14 consist of one sentence each. Each sentence contains an incorrectly used word. First, decide which is the incorrectly used word. Then, from among the options given, decide which word, when substituted for the incorrectly used word, makes the meaning of the sentence clear.
EXAMPLE:
The U.S. national income exhibits a pattern of long term deflection.
   A. reflection   B. subjection   C. rejoicing   D. growth

The word *deflection* in the sentence does not convey the meaning the sentence evidently intended to convey. The word *growth* (Answer D), when substituted for the word *deflection*, makes the meaning of the sentence clear. Accordingly, the answer to the question is D.

12. The study commissioned by the joint committee fell compassionately short of the mark and would have to be redone. 12.____
    A. successfully B. insignificantly
    C. experimentally D. woefully

13. He will not idly exploit any violation of the provisions of the order. 13.____
    A. tolerate B. refuse C. construe D. guard

14. The defendant refused to be virile and bitterly protested service. 14.____
    A. irked B. feasible C. docile D. credible

Questions 15-25.

DIRECTIONS: Questions 15 through 25 consist of short paragraphs. Each paragraph contains one word which is INCORRECTLY used because it is NOT in keeping with the meaning of the paragraph. Find the word in each paragraph which is INCORRECTLY used and then select as the answer the suggested word which should be substituted for the incorrectly used word.

SAMPLE QUESTION:
In determining who is to do the work in your unit, you will have to decide just who does what from day to day. One of your lowest responsibilities is to assign work so that everybody gets a fair share and that everyone can do his part well.
A. new   B. old   C. important   D. performance

EXPLANATION:
The word which is NOT in keeping with the meaning of the paragraph is *lowest*. This is the INCORRECTLY used word. The suggested word *important* would be in keeping with the meaning of the paragraph and should be substituted for *lowest*. Therefore, the CORRECT answer is choice C.

15. If really good practice in the elimination of preventable injuries is to be achieved and held in any establishment, top management must refuse full and definite responsibility and must apply a good share of its attention to the task. 15.____
    A. accept B. avoidable C. duties D. problem

16. Recording the human face for identification is by no means the only service performed by the camera in the field of investigation. When the trial of any issue takes place, a word picture is sought to be distorted to the court of incidents, occurrences, or events which are in dispute. 16.____
    A. appeals B. description C. portrayed D. deranged

17. In the collection of physical evidence, it cannot be emphasized too strongly that a haphazard systematic search at the scene of the crime is vital. Nothing must be overlooked. Often the only leads in a case will come from the results of this search.
    A. important
    B. investigation
    C. proof
    D. thorough

17.____

18. If an investigator has reason to suspect that the witness is mentally stable, or a habitual drunkard, he should leave no stone unturned in his investigation to determine if the witness was under the influence of liquor or drugs, or was mentally unbalanced either at the time of the occurrence to which he testified or at the time of the trial.
    A. accused
    B. clue
    C. deranged
    D. question

18.____

19. The use of records is a valuable step in crime investigation and is the main reason every department should maintain accurate reports. Crimes are not committed through the use of departmental records alone but from the use of all records, of almost every type, wherever they may be found and whenever they give any incidental information regarding the criminal.
    A. accidental
    B. necessary
    C. reported
    D. solved

19.____

20. In the years since passage of the Harrison Narcotic Act of 1914, making the possession of opium amphetamines illegal in most circumstances, drug use has become a subject of considerable scientific interest and investigation. There is at present a voluminous literature on drug use of various kinds.
    A. ingestion
    B. derivatives
    C. addiction
    D. opiates

20.____

21. Of course, the fact that criminal laws are extremely patterned in definition does not mean that the majority of persons who violate them are dealt with as criminals. Quite the contrary, for a great many forbidden acts are voluntarily engaged in within situations of privacy and go unobserved and unreported.
    A. symbolic
    B. casual
    C. scientific
    D. broad-gauged

21.____

22. The most punitive way to study punishment is to focus attention on the pattern of punitive action: to study how a penalty is applied, too study what is done to or taken from an offender.
    A. characteristic
    B. degrading
    C. objective
    D. distinguished

22.____

23. The most common forms of punishment in times past have been death, physical torture, mutilation, branding, public humiliation, fines, forfeits of property, banishment, transportation, and imprisonment. Although this list is by no means differentiated, practically every form of punishment has had several variations and applications.
    A. specific
    B. simple
    C. exhaustive
    D. characteristic

23.____

24. There is another important line of inference between ordinary and professional criminals, and that is the source from which they are recruited. The professional criminal seems to be drawn from legitimate employment and, in many instances, from parallel vocations or pursuits.
    A. demarcation   B. justification   C. superiority   D. reference

24.____

25. He took the position that the success of the program was insidious on getting additional revenue.
    A. reputed   B. contingent   C. failure   D. indeterminate

25.____

KEY (CORRECT ANSWERS)

1. A
2. B
3. B
4. C
5. D

6. C
7. D
8. D
9. A
10. C

11. D
12. D
13. A
14. C
15. A

16. C
17. D
18. C
19. D
20. B

21. D
22. C
23. C
24. A
25. B

TEST 3

DIRECTIONS: Each question or incomplete statement is followed by several suggested answers or completions. Select the one that BEST answers the question or completes the statement. *PRINT THE LETTER OF THE CORRECT ANSWER IN THE SPACE AT THE RIGHT.*

Questions 1-5.

DIRECTIONS: Questions 1 through 5 are to be answered on the basis of the following.

You are a supervising officer in an investigative unit. Earlier in the day, you directed Detectives Tom Dixon and Sal Mayo to investigate a reported assault and robbery in a liquor store within your area of jurisdiction.

Detective Dixon has submitted to you a preliminary investigative report containing the following information:

- At 1630 hours on 2/20, arrived at Joe's Liquor Store at 350 SW Avenue with Detective Mayo to investigate A & R.
- At store interviewed Rob Ladd, store manager, who stated that he and Joe Brown (store owner) had been stuck up about ten minutes prior to our arrival.
- Ladd described the robbers as male whites in their late teens or early twenties. Further stated that one of the robbers displayed what appeared to be an automatic pistol as he entered the store, and said, *Give us the money or we'll kill you.* Ladd stated that Brown then reached under the counter where he kept a loaded .38 caliber pistol. Several shots followed, and Ladd threw himself to the floor.
- The robbers fled, and Ladd didn't know if any money had been taken.
- At this point, Ladd realized that Brown was unconscious on the floor and bleeding from a head wound.
- Ambulance called by Ladd, and Brown was removed by same to General Hospital.
- Personally interviewed John White, 382 Dartmouth Place, who stated he was inside store at the time of occurrence. White states that he hid behind a wine display upon hearing someone say, *Give us the money.* He then heard shots and saw two young men run from the store to a yellow car parked at the curb. White was unable to further describe auto. States the taller of the two men drove the car away while the other sat on passenger side in front.
- Recovered three spent .38 caliber bullets from premises and delivered them to Crime Lab.
- To General Hospital at 1800 hours but unable to interview Brown, who was under sedation and suffering from shock and a laceration of the head.
- Alarm #12487 transmitted for car and occupants.
- Case Active.

Based solely on the contents of the preliminary investigation submitted by Detective Dixon, select one sentence from the following groups of sentences which is MOST accurate and is grammatically correct.

1. A. Both robbers were armed.
    B. Each of the robbers were described as a male white.
    C. Neither robber was armed.
    D. Mr. Ladd stated that one of the robbers was armed.

2. A. Mr. Brown fired three shots from his revolver.
    B. Mr. Brown was shot in the head by one of the robbers.
    C. Mr. Brown suffered a gunshot wound of the head during the course of the robbery.
    D. Mr. Brown was taken to General Hospital by ambulance.

3. A. Shots were fired after one of the robbers said, *Give us the money or we'll kill you.*
    B. After one of the robbers demanded the money from Mr. Brown, he fired a shot.
    C. The preliminary investigation indicated that although Mr. Brown did not have a license for the gun, he was justified in using deadly physical force.
    D. Mr. Brown was interviewed at General Hospital.

4. A. Each of the witnesses were customers in the store at the time of occurrence.
    B. Neither of the witnesses interviewed was the owner of the liquor store.
    C. Neither of the witnesses interviewed were the owner of the store.
    D. Neither of the witnesses was employed by Mr. Brown.

5. A. Mr. Brown arrived at General Hospital at about 5:00 P.M.
    B. Neither of the robbers was injured during the robbery.
    C. The robbery occurred at 3:30 P.M. on February 10.
    D. One of the witnesses called the ambulance.

Questions 6-10.

DIRECTIONS: Each of Questions 6 through 10 consists of information given in outline form and four sentences labeled A, B, C, and D. For each question, choose the one sentence which CORRECTLY expresses the information given in outline form and which also displays PROPER English usage.

6. Client's Name: Joanna Jones
    Number of Children: 3
    Client's Income: None
    Client's Marital Status: Single

    A. Joanna Jones is an unmarried client with three children who have no income.
    B. Joanna Jones, who is single and has no income, a client she has three children.
    C. Joanna Jones, whose three children are clients, is single and has no income.
    D. Joanna Jones, who has three children, is an unmarried client with no income.

7. Client's Name: Bertha Smith
   Number of Children: 2
   Client's Rent: $1050 per month
   Number of Rooms: 4

   A. Bertha Smith, a client, pays $1050 per month for her four rooms with two children.
   B. Client Bertha Smith has two children and pays $1050 per month for four rooms.
   C. Client Bertha Smith is paying $1050 per month for two children with four rooms.
   D. For four rooms and two children client Bertha Smith pays $1050 per month.

7.____

8. Name of Employee: Cynthia Dawes
   Number of Cases Assigned: 9
   Date Cases were Assigned: 12/16
   Number of Assigned Cases Completed: 8

   A. On December 16, employee Cynthia Dawes was assigned nine cases; she has completed eight of these cases.
   B. Cynthia Dawes, employee on December 16, assigned nine cases, completed eight.
   C. Being employed on December 16, Cynthia Dawes completed eight of nine assigned cases.
   D. Employee Cynthia Dawes, she was assigned nine cases and completed eight, on December 16.

8.____

9. Place of Audit: Broadway Center
   Names of Auditors: Paul Cahn, Raymond Perez
   Date of Audit: 11/20
   Number of Cases Audited: 41

   A. On November 20, at the Broadway Center 41 cases was audited by auditors Paul Cahn and Raymond Perez.
   B. Auditors Raymond Perez and Paul Cahn has audited 41 cases at the Broadway Center on November 20.
   C. At the Broadway Center, on November 20, auditors Paul Cahn and Raymond Perez audited 41 cases.
   D. Auditors Paul Cahn and Raymond Perez at the Broadway Center, on November 20, is auditing 41 cases.

9.____

10. Name of Client: Barbra Levine
    Client's Monthly Income: $2100
    Client's Monthly Expenses: $4520

    A. Barbra Levine is a client, her monthly income is $2100 and her monthly expenses is $4520.
    B. Barbra Levine's monthly income is $2100 and she is a client, with whose monthly expenses are $4520.

10.____

C. Barbra Levine is a client whose monthly income is $2100 and whose monthly expenses are $4520.
D. Barbra Levine, a client, is with a monthly income which is $2100 and monthly expenses which are $4520.

Questions 11-13.

DIRECTIONS: Questions 11 through 13 involve several statements of fact presented in a very simple way. These statements of fact are followed by 4 choices which attempt to incorporate all of the facts into one logical statement which is properly constructed and grammatically correct.

11. I. Mr. Brown was sweeping the sidewalk in front of his house.
    II. He was sweeping it because it was dirty.
    III. He swept the refuse into the street.
    IV. Police Officer gave him a ticket.

    Which one of the following BEST presents the information given above?
    A. Because his sidewalk was dirty, Mr. Brown received a ticket from Officer Green when he swept the refuse into the street.
    B. Police Officer Green gave Mr. Brown a ticket because his sidewalk was dirty and he swept the refuse into the street.
    C. Police Officer Green gave Mr. Brown a ticket for sweeping refuse into the street because his sidewalk was dirty.
    D. Mr. Brown, who was sweeping refuse from his dirty sidewalk into the street, was given a ticket by Police Officer Green.

11.____

12. I. Sergeant Smith radioed for help.
    II. The sergeant did so because the crowd was getting larger.
    III. It was 10:00 A.M. when he made his call.
    IV. Sergeant Smith was not in uniform at the time of occurrence.

    Which one of the following BEST presents the information given above?
    A. Sergeant Smith, although not on duty at the time, radioed for help at 10 o'clock because the crowd was getting uglier.
    B. Although not in uniform, Sergeant Smith called for help at 10:00 A.M. because the crowd was getting uglier.
    C. Sergeant Smith radioed for help at 10:00 A.M. because the crowd was getting larger.
    D. Although he was not in uniform, Sergeant Smith radioed for help at 10:00 A.M. because the crowd was getting larger.

12.____

13. I. The payroll office is open on Fridays.
    II. Paychecks are distributed from 9:00 A.M. to 12 Noon.
    III. The office is open on Fridays because that's the only day the payroll staff is available.
    IV. It is open for the specified hours in order to permit employees to cash checks at the bank during lunch hour.

13.____

The choice below which MOST clearly and accurately presents the above idea is:
A. Because the payroll office is open on Fridays from 9:00 A.M. to 12 Noon, employees can cash their checks when the payroll staff is available.
B. Because the payroll staff is only available on Fridays until noon, employees can cash their checks during their lunch hour.
C. Because the payroll staff is available only on Fridays, the office is open from 9:00 A.M. to 12 Noon to allow employees to cash their checks.
D. Because of payroll staff availability, the payroll office is open on Fridays. It is open from 9:00 A.M. to 12 Noon so that distributed paychecks can be cashed at the bank while employees are on their lunch hour.

Questions 14-16.

DIRECTIONS: In each of Questions 14 through 6, the four sentences are from a paragraph in a report. They are not in the right order. Which of the following arrangements is the BEST one?

14. I. An executive may answer a letter by writing his reply on the face of the letter itself instead of having a return letter typed.
    II. This procedure is efficient because it saves the executive's time, the typist's time, and saves office file space.
    III. Copying machines are used in small offices as well as large offices to save time and money in making brief replies to business letters.
    IV. A copy is made on a copy machine to go into the company files, while the original is mailed back to the sender.

    The CORRECT answer is:
    A. I, II, IV, III   B. I, IV, II, III   C. III, I, IV, II   D. III, IV, II, I

14.____

15. I. Most organizations favor one of the types but always include the others to a lesser degree.
    II. However, we can detect a definite trend toward greater use of symbolic control.
    III. We suggest that our local police agencies are today primarily utilizing material control.
    IV. Control can be classified into three types: physical, material, and symbolic.

    The CORRECT answer is:
    A. IV, II, III, I   B. II, I, IV, III   C. III, IV, II, I   D. IV, I, III, II

15.____

16. I. They can and do take advantage of ancient political and geographical boundaries, which often give them sanctuary from effective policy activity.
    II. This country is essentially a country of small police forces, each operating independently within the limits of its jurisdiction.
    III. The boundaries that define and limit police operations do not hinder the movement of criminals, of course.
    IV. The machinery of law enforcement in America is fragmented, complicated, and frequently overlapping.

16.____

The CORRECT answer is:
A. III, I, IV   B. II, IV, I, III   C. IV, II, III, I   D. IV, III, II, I

17. Examine the following sentence, and then choose from below the words which should be inserted in the blank spaces to produce the best sentence.
The unit has exceeded _____ goals and the employees are satisfied with _____ accomplishments.
A. their; it's   B. it's; it's   C. its; there   D. its; their

17.____

18. Examine the following sentence, and then choose from below the words which should be inserted in the blank spaces to produce the best sentence.
Research indicates that employees who _____ no opportunity for close social relationships often find their work unsatisfying, and this _____ of satisfaction often reflects itself in low production.
A. have; lack   B. have; excess   C. has; lack   D. has; excess

18.____

19. Words in a sentence must be arranged properly to make sure that the intended meaning of the sentence is clear.
The sentence below that does NOT make sense because a clause has been separated from the word on which its meaning depends is:
A. To be a good writer, clarity is necessary.
B. To be a good writer, you must write clearly.
C. You must write clearly to be a good writer.
D. Clarity is necessary to good writing.

19.____

Questions 20-21.

DIRECTIONS: Each of Questions 20 and 21 consists of a statement which contains a word (one of those underlined) that is either incorrectly used because it is not in keeping with the meaning the quotation is evidently intended to convey, or is misspelled. There is only one INCORRECT word in each quotation. Of the four underlined words, determine if the first one should be replaced by the word lettered A, the second one replaced by the word lettered B, the third one replaced by the word lettered C, or the fourth one replaced by the word lettered D.

20. The alleged killer was occasionally permitted to excercise in the corridor.
A. alledged   B. ocasionally   C. permited   D. exercise

20.____

21. Defense counsel stated, in affect, that their conduct was permissible under the First Amendment.
A. council   B. effect   C. there   D. permissable

21.____

Question 22.

DIRECTIONS: Question 22 consists of one sentence. This sentence contains an incorrectly used word. First, decide which is the incorrectly used word. Then, from among the options given, decide which word, when substituted for the incorrectly used word, makes the meaning of the sentence clear.

22. As today's violence has no single cause, so its causes have no single scheme. 22.____
    A. deference   B. cure   C. flaw   D. relevance

23. In the sentence, *A man in a light-grey suit waited thirty-five minutes in the ante-room for the all-important document*, the word IMPROPERLY hyphenated is 23.____
    A. light-grey   B. thirty-five
    C. ante-room   D. all-important

24. In the sentence, *The candidate wants to file his application for preference before it is too late*, the word *before* is used as a(n) 24.____
    A. preposition   B. subordinating conjunction
    C. pronoun   D. adverb

25. In the sentence, *The perpetrators ran from the scene*, the word *from* is a 25.____
    A. preposition   B. pronoun   C. verb   D. conjunction

KEY (CORRECT ANSWERS)

1.	D	11.	D
2.	D	12.	D
3.	A	13.	D
4.	B	14.	C
5.	D	15.	D
6.	D	16.	C
7.	B	17.	D
8.	A	18.	A
9.	C	19.	A
10.	C	20.	D

21. B
22. B
23. C
24. B
25. A

PREPARING WRITTEN MATERIAL

PARAGRAPH REARRANGEMENT
COMMENTARY

The sentences that follow are in scrambled order. You are to rearrange them in proper order and indicate the letter choice containing the correct answer at the space at the right.

Each group of sentences in this section is actually a paragraph presented in scrambled order. Each sentence in the group has a place in that paragraph; no sentence is to be left out. You are to read each group of sentences and decide upon the best order in which to put the sentences so as to form a well-organized paragraph.

The questions in this section measure the ability to solve a problem when all the facts relevant to its solution are not given.

More specifically, certain positions of responsibility and authority require the employee to discover connection between events sometimes, apparently, unrelated. In order to do this, the employee will find it necessary to correctly infer that unspecified events have probably occurred or are likely to occur. This ability becomes especially important when action must be taken on incomplete information.

Accordingly, these questions require competitors to choose among several suggested alternatives, each of which presents a different sequential arrangement of the events. Competitors must choose the MOST logical of the suggested sequences.

In order to do so, they may be required to draw on general knowledge to infer missing concepts or events that are essential to sequencing the given events. Competitors should be careful to infer only what is essential to the sequence. The plausibility of the wrong alternatives will always require the inclusion of unlikely events or of additional chains of events which are NOT essential to sequencing the given events.

It's very important to remember that you are looking for the best of the four possible choices, and that the best choice of all may not even be one of the answers you're given to choose from.

There is no one right way to solve these problems. Many people have found it helpful to first write out the order of the sentences, as they would have arranged them, on their scrap paper before looking at the possible answers. If their optimum answer is there, this can save them some time. If it isn't, this method can still give insight into solving the problem. Others find it most helpful to just go through each of the possible choices, contrasting each as they go along. You should use whatever method feels comfortable and works for you.

While most of these types of questions are not that difficult, we've added a higher percentage of the difficult type, just to give you more practice. Usually there are only one or two questions on this section that contain such subtle distinctions that you're unable to answer confidently. And you then may find yourself stuck deciding between two possible choices, neither of which you're sure about.

EXAMINATION SECTION
TEST 1

DIRECTIONS: Each question consists of several sentences which can be arranged in a logical sequence. For each question, select the choice which places the numbered sentences in the MOST logical sequence. *PRINT THE LETTER OF THE CORRECT ANSWER IN THE SPACE AT THE RIGHT.*

1.
   I. A body was found in the woods.
   II. A man proclaimed innocence.
   III. The owner of a gun was located.
   IV. A gun was traced.
   V. The owner of a gun was questioned.
   The CORRECT answer is:
   A. IV, III, V, II, I   B. II, I, IV, III, V   C. I, IV, III, V, II
   D. I, III, V, II, IV   E. I, II, IV, III, V

   1.____

2.
   I. A man is in a hunting accident.
   II. A man fell down a flight of steps.
   III. A man lost his vision in one eye.
   IV. A man broke his leg.
   V. A man had to walk with a cane.
   The CORRECT answer is:
   A. II, IV, V, I, III   B. IV, V, I, III, II   C. III, I, IV, V, II
   D. I, III, V, II, IV   E. I, III, II, IV, V

   2.____

3.
   I. A man is offered a new job.
   II. A woman is offered a new job.
   III. A man works as a waiter.
   IV. A woman works as a waitress.
   V. A woman gives notice.
   The CORRECT answer is:
   A. IV, II, V, III, I   B. IV, II, V, I, III   C. II, IV, V, III, I
   D. III, I, IV, II, V   E. IV, III, II, V, I

   3.____

4.
   I. A train let the station late.
   II. A man was late for work.
   III. A man lost his job.
   IV. Many people complained because the train was late.
   V. There was a traffic jam.
   The CORRECT answer is:
   A. V, II, I, IV, III   B. V, I, IV, II, III   C. V, I, II, IV, III
   D. I, V, IV, II, III   E. II, I, IV, V, III

   4.____

117

5.
  I. The burden of proof as to each issue is determined before trial and remains upon the same party throughout the trial.
  II. The jury is at liberty to believe one witness' testimony as against a number of contradictory witnesses.
  III. In a civil case, the party bearing the burden of proof is required to prove his contention by a fair preponderance of the evidence.
  IV. However, it must be noted that a fair preponderance of evidence does not necessarily mean a greater number of witnesses.
  V. The burden of proof is the burden which rests upon one of the parties to an action to persuade the trier of the facts, generally the jury, that a proposition he asserts is true.
  VI. If the evidence is equally balanced, or if it leaves the jury in such doubt as to be unable to decide the controversy either way, judgment must be given against the party upon whom the burden of proof rests.
  The CORRECT answer is:
  A. III, II, V, IV, I, VI   B. I, II, VI, V, III, IV   C. III, IV, V, I, II, VI
  D. V, I, III, VI, IV, II   E. I, V, III, VI, IV, II

6.
  I. If a parent is without assets and is unemployed, he cannot be convicted of the crime of non-support of a child.
  II. The term *sufficient ability* has been held to mean sufficient financial ability.
  III. It does not matter if his unemployment is by choice or unavoidable circumstances.
  IV. If he fails to take any steps at all, he may be liable to prosecution for endangering the welfare of a child.
  V. Under the penal law, a parent is responsible for the support of his minor child only if the parent is of *sufficient ability*.
  VI. An indigent parent may meet his obligation by borrowing money or by seeking aid under the provisions of the Social Welfare Law.
  The CORRECT answer is:
  A. VI, I, V, III, II, IV   B. I, III, V, II, IV, VI   C. V, II, I, III, VI, IV
  D. I, VI, IV, V, II, III   E. II, V, I, III, VI, IV

7.
  I. Consider, for example, the case of a rabble rouser who urges a group of twenty people to go out and break the windows of a nearby factory.
  II. Therefore, the law fills the indicated gap with the crime of *inciting to riot*.
  III. A person is considered guilty of inciting to riot when he urges ten or more persons to engage in tumultuous and violent conduct of a kind likely to create public alarm.
  IV. However, if he has not obtained the cooperation of at least four people, he cannot be charged with unlawful assembly.
  V. The charge of inciting to riot was added to the law to cover types of conduct which cannot be classified as either the crime of *riot* or the crime of *unlawful assembly*.
  VI. If he acquires the acquiescence of at least four of them, he is guilty of unlawful assembly even if the project does not materialize.
  The CORRECT answer is:
  A. III, V, I, VI, IV, II   B. V, I, IV, VI, II, III   C. III, IV, I, V, II, VI
  D. V, I, IV, VI, III, II   E. V, III, I, VI, IV, II

8. I. If, however, the rebuttal evidence presents an issue of credibility, it is for the jury to determine whether the presumption has, in fact, been destroyed.
    II. Once sufficient evidence to the contrary is introduced, the presumption disappears from the trial.
    III. The effect of a presumption is to place the burden upon the adversary to come forward with evidence to rebut the presumption.
    IV. When a presumption is overcome and ceases to exist in the case, the fact or facts which gave rise to the presumption still remain.
    V. Whether a presumption has been overcome is ordinarily a question for the court.
    VI. Such information may furnish a basis for a logical inference.
    The CORRECT answer is:
    A. IV, VI, II, V, I, III   B. III, II, V, I, IV, VI   C. V, III, VI, IV, II, I
    D. V, IV, I, II, VI, III   E. II, III, V, I, IV, VI

9. I. An executive may answer a letter by writing his reply on the face of the letter itself instead of having a return letter typed.
    II. This procedure is efficient because it saves the executive's time, the typist's time, and saves office file space.
    III. Copying machines are used in small offices as well as large offices to save time and money in making brief replies to business letters.
    IV. A copy is made on a copying machine to go into the company files, while the original is mailed back to the sender.
    The CORRECT answer is:
    A. I, II, IV, III   B. I, IV, II, III   C. III, I, IV, II   D. III, IV, II, I

10. I. Most organizations favor one of the types but always include the others to a lesser degree.
    II. However, we can detect a definite trend toward greater use of symbolic control.
    III. We suggest that our local police agencies are today primarily utilizing material control.
    IV. Control can be classified into three types: physical, material, and symbolic.
    The CORRECT answer is:
    A. IV, II, III, I   B. II, I, IV, III   C. III, IV, II, I   D. IV, I, III, II

11. I. Project residents had first claim to this use, followed by surrounding neighborhood children.
    II. By contrast, recreation space within the project's interior was found to be used more often by both groups.
    III. Studies of the use of project grounds in many cities showed grounds left open for public use were neglected and unused, both by residents and by members of the surrounding community.
    IV. Project residents had clearly laid claim to the play spaces, setting up and enforcing unwritten rules for use.
    V. Each group, by experience, found their activities easily disrupted by other groups, and their claim to the use of space for recreation difficult to enforce.

The CORRECT answer is:
A. IV, V, I, II, III
B. V, II, IV, III, I
C. I, IV, III, II, V
D. III, V, II, IV, I

12. I. They do not consider the problems correctable within the existing subsidy formula and social policy of accepting all eligible applicants regardless of social behavior.
    II. A recent survey, however, indicated that tenants believe these problems correctable by local housing authorities and management within the existing financial formula.
    III. Many of the problems and complaints concerning public housing management and design have created resentment between the tenant and the landlord.
    IV. This same survey indicated that administrators and managers do not agree with the tenants.
    The CORRECT answer is:
    A. II, I, III, IV   B. I, III, IV, II   C. III, II, IV, I   D. IV, II, I, III

12.____

13. I. In single-family residences, there is usually enough distance between tenants to prevent occupants from annoying one another.
    II. For example, a certain small percentage of tenant families has one or more members addicted to alcohol.
    III. While managers believe in the right of individuals to live as they choose, the manager becomes concerned when the pattern of living jeopardizes others' rights.
    IV. Still others turn night into day, staging lusty entertainments which carry on into the hours when most tenants are trying to sleep.
    V. In apartment buildings, however, tenants live so closely together that any misbehavior can result in unpleasant living conditions.
    VI. Other families engage in violent argument.
    The CORRECT answer is:
    A. III, II, V, IV, VI, I
    B. I, V, II, VI, IV, III
    C. II, V, IV, I, III, VI
    D. IV, II, V, VI, III, I

13.____

14. I. Congress made the commitment explicit in the Housing Act of 194, establishing as a national goal the realization of a *decent home and suitable environment for every American family*.
    II. The result has been that the goal of decent home and suitable environment is still as far distant as ever for the disadvantaged urban family.
    III. In spite of this action by Congress, federal housing programs have continued to be fragmented and grossly underfunded.
    IV. The passage of the National Housing Act signaled a few federal commitment to provide housing for the nation's citizens.
    The CORRECT answer is:
    A. I, IV, III, II   B. IV, I, III, II   C. IV, I, II, III   D. II, IV, I, III

14.____

15.
   I. The greater expense does not necessarily involve *exploitation*, but it is often perceived as exploitative and unfair by those who are aware of the price differences involved, but unaware of operating costs.
   II. Ghetto residents believe they are *exploited* by local merchants, and evidence substantiates some of these beliefs.
   III. However, stores in low-income areas were more likely to be small independents, which could not achieve the economies available to supermarket chains and were, therefore, more likely to charge higher prices, and the customers were more likely to buy smaller-sized packages which are more expensive per unit of measure.
   IV. A study conducted in one city showed that distinctly higher prices were charged for goods sold in ghetto stores in other areas.

   The CORRECT answer is:
   A. IV, II, I, III   B. IV, I, III, II   C. II, IV, III, I   D. II, III, IV, I

15.____

KEY (CORRECT ANSWERS)

1.	C	6.	C	11.	D
2.	E	7.	A	12.	C
3.	B	8.	B	13.	B
4.	B	9.	C	14.	B
5.	D	10.	D	15.	C

EXAMINATION SECTION

TEST 1

DIRECTIONS: Each question consists of several sentences which can be arranged in a logical sequence. For each question, select the choice which places the numbered sentences in the MOST logical sequence. *PRINT THE LETTER OF THE CORRECT ANSWER IN THE SPACE AT THE RIGHT.*

Questions 1-5.

DIRECTIONS: Read the following group of sentences and decide what would be the best order in which to put the sentences to form a well-organized paragraph. Then answer the questions below each group by putting in the space at the right the letter of the best answer according to the order you have chosen.

A. Later, it was placed first in sleds and then in carts, which were dragged by women and children to the foot of the mine shaft.
B. Gradually, mules were substituted for the women and children; and eventually steam and electricity were harnessed to the work of lifting the coal from the mine.
C. In the earliest mines it was broken loose with crude picks and thrown into baskets strapped to the backs of carriers, who toiled up and down long ladders or rough stairways.
D. The mining of coal has always meant hard labor.
E. From there, a bucket and windlass, operated by horses or mules, brought the coal to the surface.

1. If the five sentences above were rearranged in the best order, Sentence A would be placed
   A. first   B. directly after B   C. directly after C
   D. directly after D   E. directly after E

1.____

2. Sentence B would be placed
   A. first   B. directly after A   C. directly after C
   D. directly after D   E. directly after E

2.____

3. Sentence C would be placed
   A. first   B. directly after A   C. directly after B
   D. directly after D   E. directly after E

3.____

4. Sentence D would be placed
   A. first   B. directly after A   C. directly after B
   D. directly after C   E. directly after E

4.____

5. Sentence E would be placed
   A. first   B. directly after A   C. directly after C
   D. directly after C   D. directly after D

5.____

Questions 6-9.

DIRECTIONS: Read the following group of sentences and decide what would be the best order in which to put the sentences to form a well-organized paragraph. Then answer the questions below each group by putting in the space at the right the letter of the best answer according to the order you have chosen.

A. The author tried to embody in the character of his hero, Aeneas, certain qualities which characterized the Romans at their best.
B. The modern world has come to associate these ideas with the name of Aeneas.
C. The poem called the *Aeneid* was written with the purpose of setting before the Romans of the time of Augustus the ideals of life and conduct which had at one time prevailed in the Roman state and made it truly great.
D. Chief among these qualities were physical courage, skill as a warrior, ability to lead men in difficult undertakings, love of one's family and friends, unselfishness, and, particularly, devotion to the gods, and patriotism in the highest sense.

6. If the four sentences above were rearranged in the best order, Sentence A would be placed
   A. first
   B. directly after B
   C. directly after C
   D. directly after D

6._____

7. Sentence B would be placed
   A. first
   B. directly after A
   C. directly after C
   D. directly after D

7._____

8. Sentence C would be placed
   A. first
   B. directly after A
   C. directly after B
   D. directly after D

8._____

9. Sentence D would be placed
   A. first
   B. directly after A
   C. directly after B
   D. directly after C

9._____

Questions 10-13.

DIRECTIONS: Read the following group of sentences and decide what would be the best order in which to put the sentences to form a well-organized paragraph. Then answer the questions below each group by putting in the space at the right the letter of the best answer according to the order you have chosen.

A. From this point you can see tumbling mountains falling away to the north and west, and pine-covered slopes to the south.
B. It is a hike with packs and a burro over a well-made 150-mile-long trail from Giant Forest in the Sequoia National Park of California, along the new High Sierra Trail, to a spot 14,496 feet high.
C. And to the east you can look into the cavernous depths of the lowest point in the United States – Death Valley, 256 feet below sea level.

D. Reaching the top of Mount Whitney, highest point in the United States, is not the stunt of an Alpine climber.

10. If the four sentences above were rearranged in the best order, Sentence A would be placed
    A. first
    B. directly after B
    C. directly after C
    D. directly after D

    10.____

11. Sentence B would be placed
    A. first
    B. directly after A
    C. directly after C
    D. directly after D

    11.____

12. Sentence C would be placed
    A. first
    B. directly after A
    C. directly after B
    D. directly after D

    12.____

13. Sentence D would be placed
    A. first
    B. directly after A
    C. directly after B
    D. directly after C

    13.____

Questions 14-18.

DIRECTIONS: Read the following group of sentences and decide what would be the best order in which to put the sentences to form a well-organized paragraph. Then answer the questions below each group by putting in the space at the right the letter of the best answer according to the order you have chosen.

A. But even when people are told frankly that they are more easily fooled nearby, no spectator is ever so much impressed when seeing a trick on the stage as when it is done right under his nose.
B. At a distance he could watch both hands.
C. One of the many fallacies concerning sleight-of-hand is the idea that distance is an advantage to the performer.
D. Within three feet of a man you can easily divert him merely by looking him straight in the eye, or by attracting his attention to your left hand while you are doing something with the right.
E. Just the reverse is true, because angles of vision are much greater at a distance.

14. If the five sentences above were rearranged in the best order, Sentence A would be placed
    A. first
    B. directly after B
    C. directly after C
    D. directly after D
    E. directly after E

    14.____

15. Sentence B would be placed
    A. first
    B. directly after A
    C. directly after C
    D. directly after D
    E. directly after E

    15.____

16. Sentence C would be placed
    A. first
    B. directly after A
    C. directly after B
    D. directly after D
    E. directly after E

17. Sentence D would be placed
    A. first
    B. directly after A
    C. directly after B
    D. directly after C
    E. directly after E

18. Sentence E would be placed
    A. first
    B. directly after A
    C. directly after B
    D. directly after C
    E. directly after D

Questions 19-25.

DIRECTIONS: Most of the statements in Items 19 through 25 could be used in a composition about the Spanish-American War. The outline for this composition might have the following main divisions:

Topic I: Causes of the war
Topic II: Military and naval events
Topic III: Terms of the peace

Read each item and decide which one of the four lettered choices below the statement applies to that statement; then write the letter of your choice in the space at the right.

19. *Spain gave up all claim to Cuba, and recognized its independence under the protection of the United States.*
    This statement
    A. belongs to Topic I
    B. belongs to Topic II
    C. belongs to Topic III
    D. does not belong to any of these topics

20. *Fierce fighting occurred at San Juan Hill, where Colonel Theodore Roosevelt led his regiment of Rough Riders, and at El Caney.*
    This statement
    A. belongs to Topic I
    B. belongs to Topic II
    C. belongs to Topic III
    D. does not belong to any of these topics

21. *The destruction of the Spanish fleets led Spain to request peace in August 1898, after only four months of hostilities.*
    This statement
    A. belongs to Topic I
    B. belongs to Topic II
    C. belongs to Topic III
    D. does not belong to any of these topics

22. *The Hawaiian Islands lie in the Pacific Ocean some three thousand miles west of California.*
This statement
   A. belongs to Topic I
   B. belongs to Topic II
   C. belongs to Topic III
   D. does not belong to any of these topics

22.____

23. *Spain ceded Puerto Rico and Guam to the United States.*
This statement
   A. belongs to Topic I
   B. belongs to Topic II
   C. belongs to Topic III
   D. does not belong to any of these topics

23.____

24. *Americans were shocked at the cruelties inflicted on the Cubans by the government of Spain, and were in sympathy with the Cuban people.*
This statement
   A. belongs to Topic I
   B. belongs to Topic II
   C. belongs to Topic III
   D. does not belong to any of these topics

24.____

25. *Immediately upon the declaration of war in April 1898, Havana, the chief port of Cuba, was blockaded by an American fleet.*
This statement
   A. belongs to Topic I
   B. belongs to Topic II
   C. belongs to Topic III
   D. does not belong to any of these topics

25.____

Questions 26-31.

DIRECTIONS: In the outline below, certain headings have been omitted. These omissions are indicated by the numbers 26, 27, etc. First read through the outline; then answer the questions by putting the letter of the correct choice in the space at the right.

The Cultivation of Cotton

I. Conditions required for growth
   A. (26)
   B. Soil

II. Planting
   A. Preparation of soil
   B. (27)

III. (__28__)
   A. Development of stalk
   B. Development of fruit
      1. Appearance of bloom
      2. (__29__)
      3. Bursting of boll

IV. Picking of cotton
   A. Time of picking
   B. (__30__)

V. (__31__)
   A. Ginning
   B. Making bales

26. In filling in the complete outline, which one of the following would you use for *A* under heading *I*?
   A. Most important of textile products
   B. Extensive use of cotton in medicine and surgery
   C. Climate
   D. Cultivation of cotton in China, Egypt, and India
   E. Weight of bales about 500 pounds

26.____

27. Which one of the following would you use for *B* under heading *II*?
   A. Spread of cotton culture to North and West
   B. Most of world cotton crop raised in Southern states
   C. Difference between upland and sea-island cotton
   D. Dropping of seeds
   E. Long, warm summer essential to growth

27.____

28. Which one of the following would you use for heading *III*?
   A. Stages of growth
   B. Chopping (or thinning) of cotton
   C. Location of principal cotton plantations
   D. Rows usually four feet apart
   E. Average yield per acre

28.____

29. Which one of the following would you use for *B-2* under heading *III*?
   A. A soft, white fibrous substance
   B. Large yellow flowers, becoming red the second day
   C. Sandy, rather moist soil required
   D. Destruction caused by boll weevil
   E. Transition from bloom to boll

29.____

30. Which one of the following would you use for *B* under heading *IV*? 30.____
    A. Cottonseed meal used as a feed and fertilizer
    B. Picking process
    C. From August to November
    D. Types of cotton
    E. A machine to separate lint from seed

31. Which one of the following would you use for heading *V*? 31.____
    A. Preparation for shipping
    B. Importance of cotton industry to Southern economy
    C. Invention of cotton gin by Eli Whitney
    D. Principal uses of cotton
    E. Mechanical cotton picker

KEY (CORRECT ANSWERS)

1.	C	11.	D	21.	B	31.	A
2.	E	12.	B	22.	D		
3.	D	13.	A	23.	C		
4.	A	14.	B	24.	A		
5.	B	15.	D	25.	B		
6.	C	16.	A	26.	C		
7.	D	17.	E	27.	D		
8.	A	18.	D	28.	A		
9.	B	19.	C	29.	E		
10.	B	20.	B	30.	B		

www.ingramcontent.com/pod-product-compliance
Lightning Source LLC
Chambersburg PA
CBHW082208300426
44117CB00016B/2719